San Diego Christian College
2100 Greenfield Drive
El Cajon, CA 92019

Counseling
and
Marriage

RESOURCES FOR
CHRISTIAN COUNSELING

RESOURCES FOR CHRISTIAN COUNSELING

(Other volumes forthcoming)

VOLUME NINETEEN

Counseling and Marriage

DeLOSS D. FRIESEN, Ph.D.
RUBY M. FRIESEN, Ph.D.

RESOURCES FOR
CHRISTIAN COUNSELING

General Editor

Gary R. Collins, Ph.D.

WORD PUBLISHING
Dallas · London · Sydney · Singapore

Permission to quote from the following sources is gratefully acknowledged:
A Couple's Guide to Communication (p. 1), by J. Gottman, C. Notraius, J. Gonso, and H. Markman, © 1979, Champaign, Illinois. Research Press.

Adaptations of figures 10, 13, 17 from *I'm OK, You're OK* by Thomas A. Harris. © 1967, 1968, 1969 by Thomas A. Harris, M.D., Harper and Row, Publishers.

"Ten Commandments for Fighting Fair" in *Catholic Update*, © January 1988.

"Flowchart of Conflict Resolution" by Robert L. Weiss, Ph.D.

"Principle III—Client Relationship and Confidentiality" is used by permission of the Executive Director, the American Association of Pastoral Counselors.

"Principle 5, Confidentiality" is reprinted with permission from *The American Psychologist*, June 1981, © 1981 the American Psychological Association.

The "Couple 'Feeling' Word Activity," by permission of Larry Day.

Library of Congress Cataloging-in-Publication Data

Friesen, Ruby M., 1937–
    Counseling and marriage.

    (Resources for Christian counseling ; v. 19)
    Bibliography: p.
    Includes index.
    1. Marriage counseling.   2. Pastoral counseling.
I. Friesen, DeLoss D. (DeLoss David), 1937–
II. Title. III. Series.
BV4012.27.F75 1989   253.5   89-5719
ISBN 0-8499-0501-X

Printed in the United States of America

9 8 0 1 2 3 9 AGF 9 8 7 6 5 4 3 2 1

CONTENTS

v

EDITOR'S PREFACE

I WONDER IF I'M THE ONLY ONE who doesn't like weddings. When my wife and I got married, twenty-five years ago, we were grateful for the friends who came to watch as we exchanged vows. We appreciated their best wishes and congratulations. Their gifts did much to help us get started—at a time when we had lots of love but not much money. Over the years, we have watched many others begin their married lives and surely there will be frequent wedding invitations in the future.

Still, for me there is a sadness about weddings—perhaps because I have seen so many couples begin their relationships in happiness but end their marriages in bitterness, conflict, violence, and deep personal hurt. Weddings do remind us to pray for the new bride and groom. For many, their marriages will be long-lasting and fulfilling. But marriage also calls for sensitivity, mutual sharing, perpetual giving, communication, and solid hard work. Many who go to the altar fail to realize that marital fulfillment comes only to those who are committed to the marriage relationship and willing to work together to get through inevitable periods of disagreement, stress, and even boredom.

God, who created marriage shortly after he created the world, is willing to guide and strengthen those who want to build marriages that honor Christ. Often, however, there also is need for help from other believers, including counselors who are specialists in the field of marriage counseling.

DeLoss and Ruby Friesen are specialists with years of experience, both in building their own marriage and in helping many others through difficult times of marital tension.

When I was making a list of prospective authors for this series of books, I thought of several individuals who could write on marriage counseling. I was hoping, however, that I might be able to find a married couple who would be able to write this book. I dreamed of finding a husband and wife who were both professionally trained and professionally involved in marriage counseling. I also hoped for a couple who had the ability to write and who could bring fresh ideas to a topic that has been written about often. Because of the nature of this series, it was important to find committed Christians who had warm hearts for God, a clear commitment to building stronger marriages, and obvious sensitivity to their counselees.

DeLoss and Ruby Friesen met all of these goals—and more. Since they had never written a book before, they took courses in writing even as they continued their marriage-counseling practice and collected material for this new addition to the Resources for Christian Counseling series.

Like all other volumes in the series, this book is intended to be practical and helpful. Written by counseling experts, each of whom has a strong Christian commitment and extensive counseling experience, the books in this series are meant to be examples of accurate psychology and careful use of Scripture. Each is intended to have a clear evangelical perspective, careful documentation, a strong practical orientation, and freedom from the sweeping statements and undocumented rhetoric that sometimes characterize writing in the counseling field. Our goal is to provide books that are clearly written, useful, up-to-date overviews of the issues faced by contemporary Christian counselors.

All of the Resources for Christian Counseling books have similar bindings and together they are intended to comprise a helpful encyclopedia of Christian counseling.

In the months that they have been working on their manuscript, I have come to know and appreciate the warmth, sense of humility, and deep sensitivity that Ruby and Dee have brought to this project. Their book is readable, honest, illustrated with useful case histories, and intensely practical. As you read you might feel, as I did, that you are looking over the shoulders of two experienced Christian counselors who are showing us how they go about the task of rebuilding troubled marriages. They know that theological differences exist between us and admit that sometimes, despite our best efforts, marriage counseling fails and marriages break up. At such times, one can sense the authors' sadness, mixed with their continued willingness to stick by the counselees—so they don't make the same mistakes and experience the same hurts again.

The Friesens have a realistic and helpful view of marriage and marriage counseling. In the following pages you will find guidelines to help in your counseling work. And if you read carefully, you might discover, as I did, that this book includes principles that can strengthen your own marriage as well.

Gary R. Collins, Ph.D.
Kildeer, Illinois

INTRODUCTION

A few weeks after we signed the contract for this book, we watched Hugh Downs interview former President and Mrs. Jimmy Carter on "20/20." The Carters had just finished writing a book together and Rosalynn Carter said something to this effect: "Writing the book was very stressful for our marriage."

We looked at each other and we asked, "What have we gotten ourselves into?"

The decision to write a book on marriage counseling came from three desires. The first desire was to share with pastoral counselors almost thirty-two years of combined counseling experience. Pastoral counselors are that group of professionals who work with the highest number of troubled marriages. The second desire was to gain knowledge and expertise in marriage counseling. While we both counsel distressed couples, and consult with one another frequently, we believed that there was more to know and that each of us had much to teach the other. One way of finding out what the other really does in marriage counseling was to write a book together. Our third reason came from a desire for increased intimacy. Believing that the key element in intimacy is self-disclosure, we knew that writing this book would give us one more opportunity to reveal more of ourselves to each other. We feel now that we have fulfilled these three desires.

Marriage has spiritual and psychological dimensions. Together, spiritual and psychological tools help marriages to grow. The resources of prayer and Scripture study are to be used along with the psychological concepts presented in this book.

We approached the writing of this book with two questions in mind: "What are the most common problems we face in our counseling work?" and, "What would we do if a couple with one of those problems were sitting across from us right now?"

The book is organized to follow how we approach the marriage-counseling task. We repeatedly asked ourselves, "What does the counselor need to know next?" We discuss issues we believe a marriage counselor may encounter for it is our desire to give the counselor practical tools to use in counseling.

The issues discussed in the following pages are true. However, in order to protect the right to privacy of the persons involved, names and situational characteristics have been altered. In some situations we have tried to be idealistic when we could be so. In other situations we traded our idealism for pragmatism. At all times we tried to be true to what we believe the Bible says about marriage and relationships.

Was writing this book stressful to our marriage? Well, we raised our voices a few times. We argued, but we learned from one another. Most importantly, our respect and love for one another deepened. Not a bad reward.

We trust that our ideas and suggestions will reap benefits for those with whom you counsel. We hope that your own marriage will prosper as well.

Counseling and Marriage

RESOURCES FOR
CHRISTIAN COUNSELING

CHAPTER ONE

BEGINNING WITH THE COUNSELOR

What you believe has a direct effect on your behavior as a counselor. In this chapter, we ask you to consider a portion of your
beliefs—those related to a Christian marriage. Your counseling
approach will reflect your beliefs. Examine them carefully.

While we cannot react to your position on Christian marriage,
we will give you a chance to react to ours. We present here one
view of Christian marriage, which we believe integrates time-
less biblical principles with today's counseling approaches. We
don't believe that our view is the only one that may be called a
biblical view of marriage. Neither do we think it is the only one
that works. However, we believe this approach to be truthful
and workable. Our point of view has helped couples become

more cooperative and less angry and it has been helpful for couples who share biblical beliefs similar to ours; it has also helped wives and husbands who share somewhat differing biblical perspectives on marriage.

LEADERSHIP IN THE CHRISTIAN MARRIAGE

Who's the boss? Does the husband captain the team? Does the marital team have cocaptains? Or, is it more like the husband as president and the wife as vice-president? Can the wife ever be the chief executive officer?

What works in the marriage of Ruby and Dee Friesen has both theoretical/theological and practical aspects. On the theoretical/theological side we believe in a shared leadership or mutual submission approach. In practice, our day-to-day decision making is based more on our gifts, talents, interests, and who has the most time, than on our so-called roles.

Shared Leadership

We take seriously the admonitions of the fifth chapter of Ephesians: "Submit to one another out of reverence for Christ" is a call for mutual submission. While the marital roles differ and each individual's talents are unique, both partners are instructed to seriously consider the desires of the other. Ephesians 5:22 indicates that the wife is to submit herself to her husband's wishes. Ephesians 5:25 indicates that the husband is to love his wife in a sacrificial way. If the wife sincerely tries to do what her husband desires and the husband sincerely sacrifices his wants and wishes for those of his wife, what do we have? We believe we have mutual submission. The concept of mutual submission is one of the components of Genesis 2:24, "For this reason a man shall leave his father and mother and be united to his wife, and they will become one flesh." Neither person selfishly pursues his or her own needs but does what is best for the marriage and for both individuals in the marriage.

Patricia Gundry[1] presents a more detailed discussion of this in her book *Heirs Together*. Another approach to shared leadership is developed by Robbie and Donald Joy in their book *Lovers: Whatever Happened to Eden?* Robbie gives a synopsis of their concepts in an article in *Virtue* magazine entitled,

"Making Our Marriage Work."[2] In the article she states, "There are many responsibilities that we have more or less permanently delegated to each other on the basis of our gifts. Many of these look very traditional, but we do them easily and effectively because of our gifts and because we present them as gifts to each other, not because they are 'man's work' or 'woman's work.'"

Leadership by Gifts

Practically speaking, humans are not created with equal talents. We believe that leadership works best when it depends on individual gifts or strengths.

Several years ago we took a test titled The Spiritual Gifts Inventory by Gordon McMinn.[3] Among our various gifts, we discovered that one of DeLoss's stronger gifts is exhortation, while one of Ruby's stronger gifts is administration. Who then might be better at handling our day-to-day finances? Ruby would be the likely candidate. Practically speaking, she has the talent, interest, and desire to be the leader in this area of our marriage. Of course, DeLoss would support and encourage her through his gift of exhortation. He has the scriptural responsibility to be supportive—to help her carry out that leadership. We have agreed she has the responsibility to initiate and organize this area, but in no way is she responsible for doing all the work. In the chapters on communication and conflict management specific problem-solving and decision-making techniques involving both husband and wife will be presented.

Headship Leadership

Perhaps you have some strong reservations about mutual submission or shared leadership. Or, you may have a counselee who holds tightly to the belief that the husband is, in every way, the head of the house.

Some marriages operate best when the husband is the final authority. The unique talents, traits, and background of the husband and wife, in such a case, may dovetail in such a way that the marriage operates harmoniously. We are concerned, however, when a strong chain-of-command approach doesn't work for the couple.

One couple we know of was doing fine with the wife in

charge of the finances. Sharon was an accountant by profession. However, at a seminar she and Will were told that handling the finances was the husband's responsibility. Will had no talent in the financial area, but they both wanted to be obedient to what they believed to be God's will. After struggling for a year and a half, their finances in particular, and the marriage in general, were in trouble. What Will and Sharon needed was a model that allowed her to resume responsibility for the family finances while Will retained the position of leader in the family.

Couples who are troubled by the headship-leadership issue can be shown an alternative way to define this concept. We differentiate between spiritual-leadership responsibility and shared-leadership responsibility.

This diagram represents the husband's responsibility for spiritual leadership. He is placed at the top of the model. This does not imply superiority or inferiority of either marital partner, but instead shows responsibility. While much has been written on this topic, we believe the simplicity of this diagram has been beneficial for couples struggling with this issue. The most crucial element in spiritual headship is the husband's relationship with God. The husband has the responsibility to seek first the kingdom of God in his life. This is his personal issue. Not only is

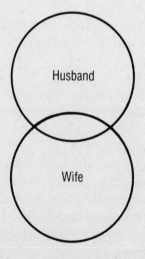

Fig. 1.1   Spiritual Leadership

he to have Jesus Christ as his Savior but he is also to put into everyday practice the Lord's truths and instructions. He creates his own personal time of spiritual study and prayer. He sets the tone for church attendance. He invites his wife's help in planning religious activities. He doesn't wait in bed Sunday morning to see if his wife is going to get up before he makes his move. If the husband presents a healthy Christian model, his wife and children will be influenced by it. This pattern is most successful when begun at the beginning of the marriage and is least successful when dad waits until his teen-age children are rebelling. Jack Wells, the father of two preschoolers, was concerned about his children's spiritual growth. Let's listen to a recent conversation with his wife, Mary.

Jack: Aren't the kids ready for more than what they are getting from their Bible storybook? How can we find out about other materials?

Mary: I'll call the Sunday School teacher. He seems to know what is available for different ages.

Jack: I would like to do some reading and discussion with them every evening, but unfortunately I have those meetings on Tuesday and Wednesday evenings.

Mary: Then those can be my nights.

This brief interaction shows us that Jack is assuming spiritual leadership in his family by taking active interest in this important area. Being a good leader, he consults with his wife. Together they collect information and work cooperatively toward the spiritual development of their children.

As the Christian writer and lecturer Kevin Leman has indicated, one can be an authority without being authoritarian. One who has authority asks for suggestions and advice and allows others to share in the decision-making process. Important tasks are delegated to, not imposed upon, others. An authoritarian leader dictates to others what is truth and how to do it.

This second diagram represents the area of practical or shared application, emphasizing equality in marriage. The husband and wife are placed on the same level. To help clients better understand the diagram, we introduce the concept of leadership by gifts. The husband can exercise his responsibility or authority in the spiritual-leadership area while both partners

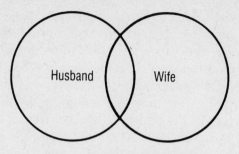

Fig. 1.2   Shared Leadership

can divide and assign practical responsibility according to time, talents, and interests.

Many couples have unrealistic and unfair expectations concerning spiritual leadership. Wives often want their husbands to lead family worship and give them spiritual instruction. While that desire is appropriate in some situations, in many it is not.

In some marriages, the wife's education and training may be greater than the husband's. More Christian books are read by women than by men, and women attend more classes in Bible studies, as a rule. Since women may have more information and training, it is unrealistic and unfair to always expect men to take a formal teaching role.

Cultural factors are influential as well. Many men are in touch with and able to share their feelings, and many are sensitive and empathic to the feelings of others. A number of men are also artistically creative. In our culture, however, these traits are more often looked for in women than in men.

Some women would like their husbands to have the spiritual insights of a seminary graduate and the emotional sensitivity of a counselor. When husbands realize this, they feel inadequate because they cannot live up to their wives' expectations.

Leadership within the Christian marriage has, at least, two variants. In the first model, spiritual leadership, the husband assumes responsibility as the spiritual head of the family. In the second model, leadership is shared. The practical tasks of family life are chosen according to the individual gifts of the husband and wife.

CHAPTER TWO

BEGINNING WITH THE COUNSELEE

Many of today's marriages are disorganized, inconsistent, and even chaotic. Neither partner is clearly designated to steer the marital ship. If a couple is presented with a navigation plan that can be clearly understood and used, the marriage and family relationship often improve. Sometimes the situation improves, not because the plan was the best possible, but because almost any plan works better than no plan at all.

A word of caution must be interjected here. It is important when counseling with any couple to respect the couple's particular views about Christian marriage. This is especially important if the couple's views differ from the counselor's. First, determine how well their approach is working for them. If it is working well, and both husband and wife endorse its principles, don't attempt to change it. If a system is working, but you think it is a distortion of scriptural principles, be patient. As the couple's relationship with you develops, perhaps the man and woman will become more open to changing their viewpoint to a more biblical one. If they have no scriptural viewpoint, gently suggest a simple approach that can be enlarged later. If there is too much emphasis on the need to believe correctly, a person may think that the pastor does not care enough about how she or he feels.

A counselor has two basic goals: (a) to teach the counselee healthy ways to handle life's problems and (b) to create a caring, supportive relationship with the counselee. Ideally, we try to satisfy both goals at the same time. When resistance is encountered, we try to apply patience.

Work on building the relationship. If persons don't feel understood and accepted, they will be likely to reject you and your counseling position along with it.

BUILDING TRUST

It was the first appointment for Helen and Ron. As she began to talk, it developed that Helen was most critical of Ron's lack of sympathy for her perspective. He never took her problems seriously enough. After listening to Helen's many complaints, I (DeLoss) shared what I was hearing and feeling. Gently, I pointed out that most of her concerns were not unusual. But I felt she was upsetting herself by her reactions to life's problems. Shortly thereafter, Helen and Ron chose to seek help from another counselor and Ron called to explain why. He thought my observations were correct, but Helen saw me as cold and unemotional, someone to whom she could not relate.

I had focused on a possible solution to the problem, but in doing so, Helen's feelings were hurt. She may have interpreted my response as meaning she was immature or that she was imagining things. It's no wonder she wanted a different counselor.

What I had said was correct; but my timing was wrong. A trusting relationship had not yet been developed. The key to building a trusting relationship is having empathy—trying to see the world through another's eyes or attempting to experience what the client experiences. We do this best by listening to the client's story. Regardless of how long, distorted, or redundant the story is, we must listen and paraphrase back what we have heard. At this stage, it is essential to hold back any comment or suggestion that might be taken as criticism.

Empathy is important in any type of counseling but it is especially so in marriage counseling. In many cases, one partner is so alienated by the spouse that empathy, sympathy, and even listening cease. The person with the problem yearns for someone who will listen.

Another element in building trust is to be warm and caring, without being possessive. You avoid possessiveness by giving the person freedom to make mistakes. You are disappointed when the counselee is disappointed—that's empathy—but you don't show disappointment when a choice is made that is contrary to one you would have made. A caring person shows acceptance without creating expectations.

After trust is established, you can introduce other sides of the issue and alternative solutions. By this time, the clients know that you care and will continue to care regardless of which decisions they make. Once trust has been established it is all right (maybe even growth producing) for the client to know that your personal position does not agree completely with his or hers. When they trust that you will continue to care for them, the real work of counseling has a good foundation.

DECIDING WHOM TO SEE

Sometimes one partner will come alone for marriage counseling. If you think the better approach for this situation is joint counseling, it is wise to move quickly in that direction in order to build rapport and trust with both spouses. Asking the person you are counseling to invite his or her partner to the next session often is enough. If your counselee believes the spouse will not come, a telephone call from you may be productive. Counselors often find a personal invitation from them is much harder to resist than a request from the spouse.

If you have counseled extensively with one spouse and joint counseling is the next step, you should consider carefully whether or not to refer the couple to another counselor. The uncounseled partner does not have the same trust level and history with you and may feel you are biased. The individual counseling relationship you have established may work against achieving productive joint counseling.

Sometimes deciding to refer is easy. The person you are counseling may emphatically state that his or her partner does not want to see you. In this case, referral is the option. In other cases, usually when the trust level between the spouses is high, the not-yet counseled partner is quite willing to join in counseling. If this feels good to both of them and you are able to shift to the *couple* as the client, go ahead.

Sometimes the decision is not as clear cut. Giving both partners the opportunity to discuss with you the counseling process and concerns they may have about marriage counseling may be necessary before a referral decision can be made.

ASSESSING THE COUPLE'S COMMITMENT TO THE MARRIAGE

If possible, we want to know by the end of the first session where each person stands in terms of commitment to the marriage. This can give the counselor a sense of appropriate direction. Our experience has shown that sometimes the hurt, anger, and disillusionment are so great, that the counselor can't proceed beyond empathic listening during the first session. Our experience has also shown that the partners in this kind of relationship may not be able to give an accurate answer to the question of commitment. If you were to chart their responses over time, you would see fluctuations in their levels of commitment.

The most accurate assessment is done over a period of time. If you have worked with a person for three months and each time you counseled you heard a desire to leave the marriage, you have an accurate picture of that person's commitment. On the other hand, many times we will hear what sounds like the death knell of a marriage during the first session, only to find after a session or two that there is, after all, a clear commitment to the marriage.

Does the level of commitment make a difference? We think it does, and we choose different counseling strategies for couples with different levels of commitment. The strategy must be carefully chosen since it can influence whether one partner decides to drop out of counseling or not. To find out where each person in the relationship thinks his or her level of commitment is, the following rating scale is beneficial:

1. Commitment, Love, but Problems.
2. Commitment, Neutral Feelings, and Problems.
3. Noncommitment, Neutral Feelings, Open to Growth.
4. Noncommitment, Negative Feelings, Closed to Growth.

An effective way to present these levels is to write out the level as you give the explanation. We speak to the clients as follows:

Couples who seek counseling are at differing places. Some are very committed to the marriage; others are not. It would be helpful to me if we can get an idea of where you are today. The following are typical levels.

Level 1. Commitment, Love but Problems. A person coming in for marriage counseling may say, "I really love my spouse and am really committed to our marriage. However, we have problems with _____. Please help us solve these problems."

Level 2. Commitment, Neutral Feelings and Problems. A person may say, "I used to love my partner and very much want to again. However, we have problems with _____. Please help us resolve these problems and regain the loving feelings."

Level 3. Noncommitment, Neutral Feelings, Open to Growth. This person might say, "I used to love my partner but I don't now. I really feel discouraged about this marriage. I don't really care whether I ever love my partner again or not. While I'm not willing to put much energy into the relationship, I wouldn't reject loving feelings if they were to return."

Level 4. Noncommitment, Negative Feelings, Closed to Growth. This person is apt to say, "Whether or not I ever loved my partner in the past is immaterial because I surely don't now. I'm not interested in working on the marriage.

11

Furthermore, if, by some strange means, feelings for my partner were to return, I would purposely crush those feelings."

After the four levels are presented and any questions are answered, the individuals are asked to choose the level that most closely describes where they are. Most see these levels as a continuum rather than four discrete points. For example, "I'm a 2 1/2" or, "I'm a 3 rapidly slipping to 4."

WHAT YOU, THE COUNSELOR, MAY EXPECT

It is common for both spouses to be at Level 1 or 2. It is rare that we see both at Level 3 and even more rare for both to be at Level 4. If both people are at Level 4, they may really be seeking "successful divorce counseling." To initiate counseling aimed at rebuilding the marriage, at least one person in the relationship has to be motivated to work on the marriage.

When two people at Level 3 come to counseling, it may be for several reasons. While each is discouraged, there still may be a desire for the marriage to work, even though the belief that the other partner can change is almost gone. Each is looking for some positive sign from the other. Another possibility (also true for two people at Level 4) is that they both want the marriage to end, but divorce violates their basic Christian beliefs. Often, these people give themselves permission to divorce after unsuccessfully counseling with the pastor. After all, they tried everything, didn't they? This explanation may be true for couples with a combination of 3 and 4 as well.

An all-too-common phenomenon is for one spouse to be at Level 1 or 2 while the other is at Level 3 or 4. One person is happy, or at least satisfied with the marriage, while the other person is quite unhappy. Happiness results from having our expectations met. In these cases, each partner has different expectations for the marriage.

Let us look at the case of Sara and Bill, who demonstrate a vast difference in their individual needs for physical attention and affection. Sara came from a home in which there was little touching and, as a wife, she desired little. Bill came into the marriage wanting a high degree of physical interaction.

Throughout twelve years of marriage Bill received little spontaneous touching from Sara. When he initiated caressing or touching, Sara frequently found his behavior annoying. In the last four years Bill has involved himself with more work and other friends to compensate for the lack of intimacy in the relationship. As a result his loving feelings have cooled. When they entered counseling, Sara claimed to be much in love with Bill; she was at Level 1. Bill, on the other hand, was unhappy with the relationship and believed he could never be happy if he stayed married to Sara. He believed she was a good person but that she could never meet his needs. He was at Level 4.

CHANGES IN LEVELS OF COMMITMENT

Occasionally, during the first few counseling sessions, the counselor may sense that one person is moving downward on the scale. For example, both partners may have agreed to do certain homework. One partner consistently tries to complete the assignment and the other finds reasons not to do so. This may be the time to suspect an extramarital affair. Nothing causes a person to move down the scale more quickly. Erosion of feelings by transferring affections from one person to another happens rapidly. Erosion of feelings by neglect takes longer.

We sometimes use the egg and basket analogy with our couples. In the deteriorating marriage all the eggs are in one basket—the marital basket. When a need goes unmet for a long period of time, its corresponding egg becomes rotten. The bad egg is removed from the basket and the feelings decrease just a bit more. This process, eggs turning bad and being removed from the basket, takes a long time. The affair is different! There are two baskets: the marital basket and the affair basket. With an affair, an egg doesn't have to go bad. The person chooses to have someone other than his or her spouse meet his or her needs. Egg after egg is taken from the marital basket and placed in the affair basket. An affair can empty the marital basket in no time!

Once you have ascertained the levels of commitment, how do you use this information? What does this mean as far as counseling strategies are concerned?

13

COUNSELING APPROACHES FOR COUPLES AT DIFFERENT LEVELS

Couples at Level 1 and 2

When counseling couples at Level 1 or 2, we have much optimism. This couple is committed. The couple wants to work. They will do mutually agreed-upon homework. Most of the time they will not sabotage the counseling. With these people we move into problem solving. More directive counseling techniques may be used since they want to know what they are doing wrong and how to change it. These couples are a joy to work with.

Beware though, if the couple stops complying with your homework assignments. Sometimes the act of seeking counseling forces one or both partners to deal more honestly with the desires for the marriage. This may result in a weaker degree of commitment. If the level of compliance changes, talk about this difference with the couple. The negative change may be temporary. If a positive response doesn't follow your discussion, it is time to reassess their individual levels of commitment to the marriage. This can help the counselor revise the counseling strategies.

One at Level 1 or 2, the Other at Level 3 or 4

It is important to give recognition to the person who wants the relationship to continue (Level 1 or 2) and has the motivation to work. This person needs to realize that having the greater motivation means he or she has the least power. The person who doesn't want the relationship, or is not sure (Level 3 or 4) has more power, because the other person is willing to do almost anything to keep the marriage. The more desperate one is, the more power the other has. Richard Stuart develops this concept of power in his book *Helping Couples Change.*[1]

It is important for the counselor to establish a good working relationship with the person who is more powerful. All too often the pastor, because of a strong, shared belief in saving the marriage, forms the better counseling relationship with the less powerful partner. As a result, the person with greater power becomes alienated and frequently leaves counseling. It may be useful to share privately with the less powerful partner that you, the counselor, will be focusing on the problems and feelings of the other partner at this initial stage. Before you can have an influence on people at Level 3 or 4, they must see you as understanding and accepting them in their situation. Therefore, the spouse at Level 1 or 2 must understand the importance of a nonpressured atmosphere, a setting in which the partner is not forced to make a decision.

The person at Level 3 or 4 is discouraged about the relationship. If the discouragement results from deterioration of the marriage, rather than from an affair, we use the models Falling Out of Love and Falling Back in Love. These models (presented in chapter 4) are designed to encourage those who are discouraged to keep trying.

Couples at Level 3 or 4

While it is rare for these couples to seek counseling, they occasionally do. Since neither person has much commitment to working on the marriage, it is necessary to help them define an alternative counseling goal.

Some of these couples have a strong commitment to the idea of marriage even though they have little energy for working on their own marriages. People often tell us they have worked hard and just can't do it any more. When someone says he or she has worked on the marriage, we often ask whether the partners have worked on the problems together, at the same time, or whether they have worked on them independently. The answer often is, "I worked on it by myself."

A partner may think he or she is free to terminate a poor marriage with a clear conscience if great effort has been expended. In counseling, we don't want to reinforce this belief; we want to do just the opposite. Secondly, we believe the couple makes more progress when the partners work together. When each works in isolation, the other partner doesn't know what to look for or what reaction is wanted. It is all too easy to give up and revert to old patterns when working solo.

It is also possible the couple has tried to correct something that may not be the underlying cause for the problems. Sometimes a professional is required to help see clearly what the

15

problem is and how to handle it. For some couples, it may be useful to state:

Working alone to solve marital problems is hard, frustrating work. Usually people give up before they have made any real headway. It is easy to get discouraged and disillusioned about the marriage. You now have an opportunity to work on the marriage together. This kind of work has the most payoff. If, after some concentrated effort on both of your parts to rebuild the marriage, something positive doesn't happen, you can reevaluate your situation. At least then you will know you both sought professional help and you both worked on it together.

Couples who are both at Level 4 have the right to expect the counselor to explore with them questions such as the following:

—How have you arrived at this decision?
—Is there anything the other person could do that would make a difference?
—What do you think you contributed, or didn't contribute, that brought you to this point?
—Have you done all that you need to do to protect your personal integrity?
—What do you hope to accomplish by leaving this relationship?
—Why do you think this accomplishment was absent in this relationship?

Some Christians might feel that the previous paragraphs give people an excuse to divorce. It is true that there is some risk in this approach. Such a risk, however, is similar to the risk of surgery. There is certain risk if surgery is not done and certain risk if surgery is done. If death is almost certain unless medical intervention takes place, a dangerous surgical procedure is still the better option.

Quite often the couple at Level 3 or 4 comes to counseling as a last-ditch effort. If you cannot persuade them to work on their relationship with you, a marriage fatality is a strong possibility.

We believe that if both people actively participate in counseling and practice the principles taught, the relationship and their feelings can improve.

Other couples at Level 3 or 4 lack motivation to work on the relationship. They are willing, however, to explore what went wrong. They want to understand the breakdown of their marriage and to have help in dissolving the relationship in the least hurtful manner. Some plan to be in another relationship in the future and don't want to repeat their mistakes. If a person comes only because he or she promised parents, kids, or pastor one visit to the counselor, we use the "understanding-of-what-went-wrong" reason for continuing counseling. This person doesn't want to cause his or her partner to believe that improving the marriage is the focus of being there. For some, this reluctance to mislead the other partner is very strong. This needs to be recognized and accepted by the counselor. It may be helpful to assist the other partner in recognizing this fact as well. We sometimes say to the less powerful partner, "If you value the potential for what could be in the marriage, it is important to be patient. Your partner does not want to give you false hope. Pressuring your partner at this time will probably work against you."

A second approach for the couple who is determined to divorce is lack of opposition. They are prepared for your resistance, but not for your cooperation. If you said, "I'm in favor of keeping the marriage you have. I believe there are techniques you haven't learned. However, I see that from your view, things are bleak. You both believe you have an unsuccessful marriage. Since you won't be persuaded not to divorce, then let us work on making the divorce a successful one."

What is a successful divorce? We believe this is a divorce in which there is open communication and a spirit of compromise. These skills are necessary to divide property and to deal with custody issues and shared parenting. In addition, we feel that if a couple is able to develop relationship skills with each other for a successful divorce, they may decide that perhaps they could have a successful marriage after all.

With a person or couple at Level 3 or 4, we tread carefully. If there is any resistance to directly working on the marriage, we move to the indirect approach. As Christians, this is difficult since we would like to see every couple committed to rebuilding the marriage. If a dogmatic Christian's ABSOLUTELY CAN'T DIVORCE stance is taken, we believe most discouraged clients will drop out of counseling. Some Christian counselors feel it is better to have firm standards even if the clients rejects those standards. We, however, are more concerned about the number of couples who finally decide to keep and build their marriages than we are about imposing rigid standards.

We find that openly discussing divorce doesn't encourage divorce. When a client discusses divorce with us, we know that negative as well as positive issues are being examined. If divorce is discussed only with already-divorced friends, the bias is obviously in the other direction. Isn't it better that they discuss the possibility of divorce with you?

CHAPTER THREE

INDIVIDUAL APPROACH VS. SYSTEMS APPROACH

WHICH ONE IS CORRECT FOR MARRIAGE COUNSELING?

The term *individual psychotherapy* denotes various theories and techniques used in therapy with individuals. These focus on creating some kind of change in the individual counselee who may explore such diverse areas as childhood memories, unrealistic expectations, or poor methods of time management. The approach may stress insight, rational thinking, or positive behavior change. The individual, with the help of the therapist, has the responsibility for change. Much of the therapy is internal, with changes in thinking patterns leading to changes in feelings and behaviors.

If you were to counsel couples the way you do individuals, the spouses would be seen separately. Your counseling focus would be more on a person's feelings and personal issues than on the interaction between two people.

Does this mean we are opposed to the individual approach? Not in the least! We do not advocate the sacrifice of individual growth and integrity to save a marriage. However, we believe that by using an integrated approach both the individual and the marriage can grow. But, before we commit ourselves, let's take a look at systems approaches to psychotherapy.

SYSTEMS APPROACH TO PSYCHOTHERAPY

Jay Haley states, "Marriage therapy tended to follow the current ideas developed in other therapies. When psycho-dynamic theory was popular, marriage counselors tended to see spouses individually and to explore the influences of their pasts on their present marriages. . . . When behavior therapy ideas became prominent in the individual therapy field, marriage therapists began to change toward encouraging positive reinforcements and became more concerned with current behavior rather than the past. When family therapy became popular, marriage therapists began to see spouses together and to think of a marriage as part of a larger system. During this period therapists were trying to break free of individual descriptions. Couples were viewed as interacting systems, as rule-governed entities, or as conditioning systems in which what one person did reinforced what the other did."[1]

A system is a relational unit of more than one person. Typically, we think of the system unit as having definite boundaries (i.e., certain people are included and certain people are excluded). Who is included and who is not is determined by the interaction and interdependency of the various people in that unit. In most cases, all persons living under the same roof would be members of the unit. Others, grown children or in-laws, are sometimes included as well.

Most family therapy uses a systemic approach. The whole family, or family system, is the patient. In marriage counseling, if more than just the husband and wife make up the family unit, then only part of the family is the patient.

Who gets included in the system or family unit is only part of what defines a systems approach. The most important aspect of the system is that it is dynamic and interactive. If one person in the marriage system changes, the whole system changes. The authors of *Milan Systemic Family Therapy* state:

> One person's attempt to establish control leads to another person [*sic*] feeling threatened and trying in turn to establish control. An endless game ensues where no one can clearly win or lose.[2]

Individual psychotherapy is not likely to bring an end to this game. It is important to see the couple as a unit or system, at least part of the time. Both partners need to understand how the behavior of one can affect the behavior of the other.

Both of us work with many people on an individual basis. They are seen as individuals even though we know that others affect their lives. When we work with a couple, our perspective changes.

We believe that the behavior of one person affects the behavior of another. The problems that we face in marital counseling propel us to the research and clinical experience of other marital therapists. We want to know how the behavior of one spouse affects the behavior of the other. Several writers have helped us in this understanding.

The concept of systems psychotherapy is often seen in writings that do not arise from a strict systems approach. Margaret and Jordan Paul, in their book *Do I Have to Give Up Me to be Loved by You,*[3] describe four different kinds of couples: control-control, control-compliant, control-indifferent, and indifferent-indifferent. The authors' focus is on the pattern of the specific couple, not the characteristics of the individuals.

David Viscott, in *I Love You, Let's Work It Out*, talks about three types of individuals: dependent, controlling, and competitive. If you view this through an individual psychology approach, you only deal with three types. A couple, however, is more complex; it is a system. Viscott describes six different types of couples: controlling-controlling, controlling-dependent, controlling-competitive, dependent-dependent, dependent-competitive, and competitive-competitive.[4]

Ellyn Bader and Peter Pearson combine object-relations

theory and systems. They look at the developmental stages of the couple—symbiotic, differentiating, practicing, and individuation—to determine the most appropriate counseling intervention. They see a similarity to the same stages an infant goes through to separate from its mother. As the infant and mother must become comfortable with a reasonable amount both of closeness and separateness (differentiating and practicing) from each other, so must the partners in a marriage relationship. The partners need to be comfortable being both separate and together.[5]

James Dobson discusses this notion in his film series, "Turn Your Heart Toward Home," labeling the process of moving closer together and then moving farther apart as marital breathing.[6] This movement back and forth is normal and healthy in the marital relationship.

MARITAL CONTRACT AS A SYSTEM

Clifford Sager applies a different twist for understanding marriage dynamics, using the systems approach. Sager believes all relationships, especially marriage, are contractual. A contract is an agreement that one person will provide certain goods, services, attitudes, and behaviors in exchange for the other person's providing certain goods, services, attitudes or behaviors.[7]

In a business contract the obligations of both parties are understood by both, and terms are agreed upon by both. A seafood wholesaler agrees to sell a thousand pounds of fresh, grade A fish for two thousand dollars (two dollars a pound). If at the time of delivery, the buyer only brings $1500 the seller would be within his rights to deliver only 750 pounds. Or if the fish turns out to be grade A frozen rather than fresh, the buyer would be within his rights to refuse the delivery or only pay fair market value for frozen fish.

Relational contracts are quite similar in theory, but in practice they often yield quite different results. Relational contracts are similar in that if one keeps his end of the bargain, the other keeps his, and vice versa, if one changes the deal, the other will also. This is really the essence of the system concept. If one person changes, it alters the system and leads to changes in the other person.

Unfortunately, once a person begins to change, a vicious cycle may begin. A wife thinks her husband is spending too much money. To compensate, she spends less on food and household items. Her frugality irritates her husband and he is even less careful with spending. This causes her to pull the financial reins even tighter. It can go back and forth, on and on—a no-win situation for both.

Business contracts and relational contracts differ in one important way. In business, both people know the terms and conditions. Each side has a chance to agree or renegotiate. In relational contracts, it is possible to not even know a contract is in effect.

George and Marti had both been widowed. Both had children but the kids were pretty much on their own. During their year-long courtship, George and Marti squeezed out time for each other from demanding and successful careers. Marti had her aging but independent father living with her. As they approached marriage several assumptions were important to them. The first was that Marti assumed her dad would always live with them. (This assumption had only casually been discussed.) A second assumption was that they would live in George's house since it was quite a bit larger than Marti's. (This assumption was discussed and agreed upon.) Thirdly, George assumed Marti would continue working. George thought that if he and Marti both worked hard for a few more years they would both be able to retire early. (This assumption was never discussed.) Marti assumed that since George's first wife didn't work and since she worked only out of necessity, she would not work after they married.

During the early part of the courtship George had been more than friendly to Marti's dad. When the wedding was about a month away, Marti announced that she was quitting her job early rather than doing it after the wedding. Since they didn't actually need her salary, George didn't say anything. She was so excited by the wedding and her new life, George didn't want to spoil her fun. Shortly thereafter though, George began to have second thoughts about his father-in-law living with them. He shared those concerns with Marti. The closeness that Marti had felt for George since the early months of their relationship began to erode.

In the example, we can see that George had a conscious but unspoken contract. "If you will continue your career for the next five years or so I will be happy to have your dad stay with us. If you don't work and your dad stays with us, I get the feeling I'm taking care of two people at my expense. Some of the things I like about you are your independence and your industry."

When Marti quit work George changed his response, although it was not to be mean or to get even. Marti hadn't honored the contract. This was a one-way contract. George wanted it, believed it, and acted as if it were fully agreed upon by Marti (Marti was unaware of the contract). A one-way contract is as powerful to the person originating it, as a mutually agreed-upon, two-way contract. If George and Marti had openly discussed each of their wants and expectations, false assumptions would not have been made. If she had understood George's reasoning and logic early, before her desires had solidified into expectations, Marti might have been willing to continue her career.

Note the vicious-cycle nature of the interaction. A change in Marti's work plans led to a change in George's attitude about his father-in-law living with them. George's change in attitude led to a change in Marti's affection toward George. Our example stops here but in real life it can go on and on with each action and reaction increasing the distance between the partners.

His Needs, Her Needs

In his book *His Needs, Her Needs,* Willard Harley presents a position similar to Sager's. He believes that people have specific needs; if we have our needs met, we are much more likely to work at meeting the other's needs; if our needs are not met, we will begin to meet fewer and fewer of our partner's needs. Harley believes a woman has a greater need for conversation with her husband and a man has a greater need for recreational companionship from his wife. If, for example, the wife puts a high priority on doing things with her husband that he enjoys, she is much more likely to get the conversation she desires.[8]

THE MARITAL WAGON: AN INTEGRATED LOOK AT MARITAL COUNSELING

To describe the relationship between individual and systems issues in the marriage, we often use this analogy. Each person has a wagon. On this wagon is a treasure chest full of jewels and a garbage can full of garbage. The jewels represent our positive traits and the garbage our negative traits. When we get married we each move our treasure chests and garbage cans onto a new wagon—the marital wagon. In addition to the individual treasure chests and garbage cans, we now have a marital treasure chest and a marital garbage can. This treasure chest is filled with our joys, successes, and happy times. The marital garbage can is filled with our fights and disappointments. A couple is in trouble when there are too few items in the treasure chests and too many in the garbage cans.

When the couple comes to us we inspect all the treasure chests and garbage cans. With a few couples, the individual garbage cans are nearly empty and each partner has a lot of treasures. As individuals, they are pretty healthy, but as a couple there are real problems. In this case, we see them only as a couple in therapy; we do not see them on an individual basis, for it is the marital garbage can that needs emptying and the marital treasure chest that is in need of filling.

Other couples may present full individual garbage cans along with a full marital one. Doing some individual work is a prerequisite in assisting this couple to improve. Here, individual counseling and testing is very helpful. When the individual issues that negatively affect the marriage have been dealt with then the primary focus can shift to marriage counseling.

Summary

When marriage counseling begins, your clients will be best served if you view their relationship as a system. You are treating the couple, the relationship, and the interaction. Your technique will reflect the notions of reciprocity—a change in one causes a change in the other. Your assessment procedure will examine the relationship process, rather than attempt to predict the relationship outcome.

Be aware that in addition to the couple history and personality, you also have two individuals with their own histories and personalities. At times, dealing with individual issues must come before dealing with couple issues. If this is the case then an appropriate individual psychotherapy model is used. When you are ready to move to couple issues, it is clearly beneficial to view the couple as an interactive unit. In the system concept, the whole is greater than the sum of the parts.

CHAPTER FOUR

SETTING THE STRUCTURE
FOR HOPE

Pastor Smith sat quietly listening as the young couple voiced their discouragement. Tom felt like he had lived with disappointment all his married life and things were not going to change for the better. He was thinking that separation might be a good idea.

Sue stated that she loved Tom. She did not think separation was the answer. However, she felt they did not know how to recreate the romantic feelings they once had. She ended by saying that Tom entertains fantasies involving the women in his office; she guesses she is not very exciting to him.

BUILDING HOPE

Often when couples seek marriage counseling they are discouraged and disillusioned. It is useful to address this fact in order to build motivation and hope. This chapter presents tools for accomplishing this task.

Reuben Hill has reported Koos's investigation of the happiness level of couples before and after a major crisis.[1] A crisis can cause the couple to join forces against a common problem. The couples reported that after a crisis the level of happiness increased for those who were motivated to work on the marriage relationship. We show couples Figure 4.1:

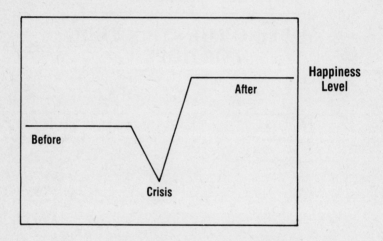

Fig. 4.1   Happiness Levels Before and After Major Crises

The horizontal line represents the happiness level of the couple. It is encouraging for couples to see graphically that things can be better.

Many people feel that if loving feelings are lost they cannot be regained. During the initial stages of counseling, it is useful for the counselor to debunk this myth and point out to the couple that love can be rebuilt. Many couples will give the marriage another try if only they can believe that loving feelings might return.

FALLING OUT OF LOVE—FALLING BACK IN LOVE

We have created and used a technique that graphically shows the patterns of Falling Out of Love and Falling Back in Love.[2] Falling Out of Love is shown to the couple first because it is a historical fact with which the counselee can identify. In addition, there are psychological principles found in the Falling Out of Love phase. If people can see the Falling Out of Love section as true, they are much more likely to concede that the Falling Back in Love notion might also be true.

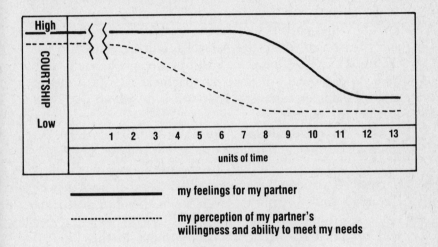

my feelings for my partner

-------------------------- my perception of my partner's willingness and ability to meet my needs

Fig. 4.2   Falling Out of Love Model

We explain Figure 4.2 to the couple in this way. The solid line represents your feelings for your partner. These feelings are usually thought of in a romantic sense, but they include friendship and commitment as well. The dotted line represents your perceptions or beliefs of your partner's willingness and ability to meet your needs. These beliefs are largely based on what your partner does and says.

The courtship period begins on the left side of the graph. Both the dotted (how you perceive your partner's behavior) and the solid (your feelings) lines are high. There are strong

29

feelings and your partner is perceived as meeting your love needs. Most of us get married at this point.

During courtship two factors are operating. One is that your partner is trying to make a good impression. This is not phony. One person really wants to do those things that are pleasing to the other. The second factor is the relative lack of conflict in the relationship. This means that, for the most part, you give your partner the benefit of the doubt. Even if a behavior occurs that could be interpreted negatively, you do not choose to do so. After the honeymoon, things change. We drop our guard. We often return to the kind of living patterns we had in our families of origin, in the dormitories, or in the barracks. During courtship not only was the best foot forward, but we spent much more time on our object of love, our partner, and less time on other friends or interests. Even work or school were put on the back burner.

After marriage, life falls into a more normal pattern and some of the neglected activities are resumed. This can't happen without spending less focused time with one's partner. If expectations are realistic, and if each places the other first in priority, even when spending less time together, things are fine. Your feelings for your partner will remain high. There is contentment in this kind of marriage.

Many marriages are not so fortunate. So, let's return to "Falling Out of Love" and follow what happens when things deteriorate. The two lines on the graph start out high and then are broken by jagged vertical lines. The period of time between courtship and the changes in perception varies. It can happen on the honeymoon or it can take twenty years. The highest occurrence of divorce is in the second year of marriage. This suggests that deterioration may begin within days of the wedding. By the third time unit on the graph, one partner perceives that the other is meeting fewer needs than were met earlier in the relationship. For example, your spouse may spend less time with you and more time with friends. However, your feelings of love remain high. At the sixth time unit, your partner is meeting significantly fewer of your needs but your love is still high. Why is this so?

Early in a love relationship, before discouragement sets in, we make excuses to explain what is happening. We blame our marital difficulties on such things as the adjustment of early marriage, lack of money, and crowded living conditions. We are sure it will be different when (a) he finishes school, (b) she has the baby, (c) we move back to our hometown, (d) she gets a raise, or (e) the youngest child starts school. We experience many events or changes that produce stress, and we believe that when the stress passes, things will improve. There is some truth to this. Sometimes things *are* rough because of stress, and when stress passes, things improve.

For a while, sometimes a very long while, you give your relationship the benefit of the doubt. But if stresses come and go and your partner still doesn't meet your needs, your feelings change. Eventually, your feelings begin to follow the course of your partner's behavior (or at least your view of that behavior). At the eighth time unit on the graph, your feelings have begun to deteriorate. This deterioration proceeds rapidly until, at the thirteenth time unit, the feelings and perceptions are lined up together. Now both levels are low.

To summarize the Falling Out of Love diagram, the dotted line stands for perception of one partner's willingness and ability to meet the needs of the other. This view is partially internal; it is an interpretation of the partner's behavior. The interpretation may be misguided. Perhaps one partner is too sensitive and distorts the meaning of the behavior. Good aspects may be overlooked while the negative ones are emphasized. However, much of this interpretation does result from the spouse's behavior. If the spouse shows loving, respectful, courteous, unselfish behavior in a consistent fashion, the partner very likely is perceived as willing and able to meet needs. In a large measure then, we use the dotted line to represent the behavior of one person, while the solid line represents the feelings of the other.

This model illustrates two psychological principles. First, *feelings are tied to behavior*. More accurately, "I see and think about your behavior, and those thoughts produce my feelings." Second, *changes in feelings lag behind changes in behavior*. Again, "I see your behavior, and I think about your behavior, but my thoughts contain certain excuses or reasons why you are behaving as you do. Therefore, as long as my thoughts excuse you, my feelings are still positive or hopeful. Eventually, I'm thinking of your behavior as very unfulfilling to me and my love feelings begin to disappear."

The position at the far right of the Falling Out of Love model (both the solid and dotted lines at the bottom) is the condition many couples reach prior to seeking counseling. At least one partner, if not both, will have feelings and partner perception at the low end of the scale.

When we sense the man and woman understand these concepts and can relate them to their marriage, we move on to the Falling Back in Love step.

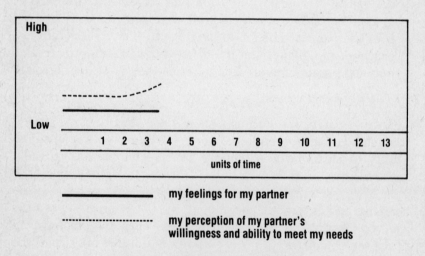

Fig. 4.3 Falling Back in Love Model

We describe the Falling Back in Love model from a discouraged client's point of view.

The first stage of the model shows, at the first time unit, that your perception of your partner's behavior is low. Also your feelings are low. The counseling intervention begins here. Early in counseling, problems are discussed (second time unit). Several sessions and weeks pass, (third time unit) and your partner shows a slight behavior change. However, your feelings remain low.

Why don't your feelings change? After all, your partner's behavior changed. In all probability, you haven't changed your feelings because you doubt your partner's sincerity. At the beginning (first time unit), your partner's behavior is low. After all, if this person really cared about you and the marriage, there would have been changes a long time ago. You're really skeptical. You are not even sure why your partner is here. Maybe your partner wants the marriage to continue for security reasons, but does he or she really want to change?

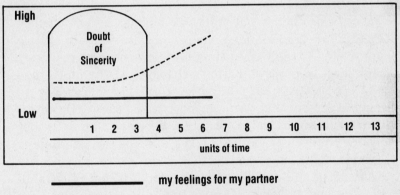

Fig. 4.4 Falling Out of Love—Doubt of Sincerity Model

DOUBT OF SINCERITY

The next version of the graph shows an overlay labeled, the Doubt of Sincerity. Counseling continues—let's see what happens.

At the fourth time unit, you no longer doubt the sincerity of your partner, but your feelings do not change. Nor do the feelings change at unit 5 or 6. If doubt of sincerity is not the problem, what is? You now believe your partner wants to change but you don't think your partner is *able* to change—you don't think change is really possible. Isn't it reasonable to assume that if change were possible, it would have already occurred? At the fourth time unit, you were sure your partner wasn't able to change. Now you begin to consider the evidence that your partner has consistently worked on making the change.

DOUBT OF ABILITY

The next version of the graph shows an overlay labeled, Doubt of Ability. Counseling continues—again let's see what happens.

At the seventh time unit you no longer doubt your partner's sincerity or ability, but still your feelings do not change. As counseling continues, your partner continues to change positively. At the eighth time unit your partner reaches a high level of positive marital behaviors. At the ninth time unit the behavior has not improved further but it does remain at a level that was previously satisfactory. However, your feelings *still haven't changed*. Even at unit 8 or 9, your feelings didn't change. Why? The same factors continue to operate. This time, however, it is not doubt of sincerity or doubt of ability. This time, the doubt is that of durability. You now believe that your spouse is sincere and able, but you don't think the behavior change will last. You fear that your partner's motivation is only to get you to stay in the marriage.

You don't think your partner will maintain the change once you commit yourself to staying. You are also afraid to begin to feel again. If you have no feelings, then you can leave the marriage with less emotional pain. But if you fall back in love with your partner, you become vulnerable. You can be hurt again.

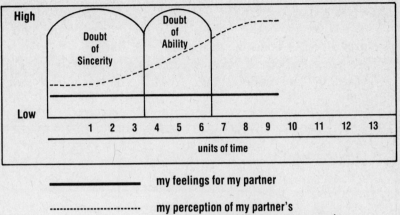

my feelings for my partner

········· my perception of my partner's
willingness and ability to meet my needs

Fig. 4.5   Falling Out of Love—Doubt of Ability Model

This resistance to a change of feelings is natural. It is a God-given emotional protection mechanism. Another way of looking at this is to think of it as a trust issue. It takes a while for a high level of trust to be destroyed. But once it is destroyed, it takes a long time to rebuild trust.

Often at this point in the counseling process, further discouragement occurs. We find it useful to actively help the partners understand that this is an aspect of the change process.

We use the Falling Back in Love model to help set realistic marriage-counseling expectations for you. There is a tendency for the partner who is doing the changing to become discouraged. All that work and no positive response. We caution against asking any of these dead-end questions: "Well, how do you feel now?" or, "Do you love me just a little?" or, "It's been three months since we started counseling; haven't your feelings changed yet?" The person whose feelings are at a low level also tends to be discouraged. "My partner is working so hard, but nothing is helping. My feelings haven't changed. Maybe we should end this misery."

DOUBT OF DURABILITY

The next version of the graph adds another overlay: the Doubt of Durability. We continue to speak to the couple.

We encourage both of you to keep trying. There is hope. This last stage of the model shows what is likely to happen at this point.

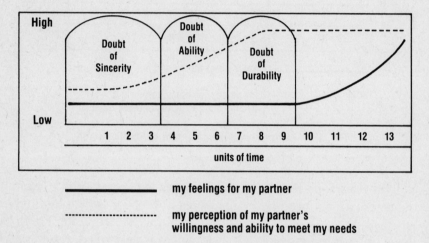

my feelings for my partner

my perception of my partner's willingness and ability to meet my needs

Fig. 4.6   Falling Back in Love—Doubt of Durability Model

After the doubt of durability has been crossed and the basic elements of trust have been reestablished, the positive feelings will slowly begin to return. In other words, if your partner, as represented by the dotted lines, adequately maintains the loving and positive behavior, your feelings slowly, and intermittently, begin to move to higher levels.

Most couples in discouraged relationships take from six to twelve months to reach the point at unit 10 where feelings begin to change. It can take another year or more to reach higher, more positive levels. But *it can happen.* Love feelings can be rekindled. This is the main message we want to impart. We want to destroy the myth that says that once loving feelings are gone, it is all over. We, and many of our clients say, *not so!*

WHEN THE MODELS DON'T WORK

We have focused on the couple in which one partner has low feelings and the other partner is motivated to change. We have seen a few couples where both have low feelings and yet both are willing to change, at least enough to see if something positive can be made of their marriage. This kind of marriage requires the same counseling procedure and process as above. However, the process takes more time.

Sometimes, the person with the low feelings is right. The partner is sincere but isn't able to change. Or, we see people who are more scared than sincere. The changes made are not long-term ones; they occur only to placate the dissatisfied partner. These marriages fail.

There is another kind of unhappy ending. Once in a while, the partner motivated to change realizes his or her mistakes in the marriage and gives it a genuine try. Change is made and persistently maintained. The dissatisfied partner never recovers his or her feelings. What has gone wrong here? Is the theory or the model wrong? We find the model so universally useful that we use it as if it were a scientific law. However, the model doesn't fit every situation. Some people quench any positive feelings that surface and thus negate any attempt at rebuilding.

Is it possible that a person can be so badly hurt for such a long period of time that recovery is impossible? Can love in some cases be so dead that it can't be resurrected? Theologically, in terms of grace and forgiveness, we say no! However, by acknowledging human weaknesses and imperfections, we arrive at a different answer. At times we find a situation in which, even after one partner achieves genuine changes, the other person can't (or at least, doesn't) begin to trust again. The history of destructive behavior is too strong to be overcome.

A Word of Caution

You have just read the directions but you are not yet ready to use the tool. Because this technique is somewhat involved, we encourage you, the counselor, to practice explaining this technique. Show it to a colleague or your spouse before using it with clients. Practice tailoring this to fit your style and you will find it will flow quite naturally. Without practice you could experience unnecessary failure with some of your first couples.

Day-to-Day Use of the Model

In our day-to-day counseling, we seldom present the models and graphs in their entirety with a couple who is already committed to working on the marriage. We may, however, present a shortened version to emphasize the importance of consistently following through with the agreed-upon changes over long periods of time. We also emphasize the need for patience. Most problems didn't emerge in a day, and any change will take time. For couples with at least one discouraged partner who believes the marriage is probably over, we present the entire model as soon as possible.

The timing of the presentation depends on the needs of the clients. We begin every counseling relationship with an invitation for the client to tell his or her story. For some clients, that takes only fifteen or twenty minutes, and then they are ready to hear what we have to say. Other clients need three to five sessions before they are ready. In practice, many discouraged clients are shown the model in the first or second session. Most of the remainder will not see it until the fourth or fifth session.

In some ways, presenting the model is not the beginning of counseling. It is, in and of itself, not a treatment strategy since it will not change feelings about a client's partner. It may, however, change a client's feelings about marriage counseling. What we are hoping for is increased willingness to engage in counseling.

It is best if you can elicit agreement from both people to work on the marriage. People work harder when they give a verbal commitment to do so. We will accept as a substitute, however, a client's willingness to come for counseling. Sometimes a client won't promise to work on the marriage, but he or she will agree to come back next week for another counseling session.

Summary

The primary purpose of using the Falling Out of Love and Falling Back in Love models is to build hope in a relationship that looks bleak. Every couple, at least in the beginning, wants to have a happy marriage. It requires faith, however, to believe that even though I am not happy now, if my partner and I do the right things, I can be happy in the future. By using these models, taking the chance becomes more an act of reasoned faith than one of blind faith.

The following chapters discuss tools and strategies to use in counseling once the couple has agreed to work on the relationship.

CHAPTER FIVE

WHAT NEXT? DECISION STRATEGIES FOR THE COUNSELOR

Pastor Smith listened intently as Andrea listed all of the things her husband had not done right. "We have two children. The oldest will be two next month and the baby is nine months old. Our house is too small and the kids share a bedroom. When I have to get up to feed the baby, our oldest son wakes up and won't go back to sleep. The baby cries a lot. Ed can't make either of the children settle down. He works as a janitor and gets paid an hourly wage. We don't have enough money. He doesn't want to try to get a better job. He doesn't try to help with the kids. When I get frustrated, he doesn't want me to call him at work. I can't stand this. I don't know, I guess he just doesn't have any ambition." Throughout Andrea's harangue, Ed was silent, occasionally, shifting from side to side in his chair.

Meanwhile, Pastor Smith couldn't help thinking, *the reason they've come to counseling is so I can make the husband change.*

It is not uncommon for the counselor to encounter such a beginning. As a counselor, you will want to determine right away what are realistic counseling expectations for you and for the persons you counsel.

Let's start by looking at realistic expectations for you.

- You can't save all marriages. Psychiatrist Harvey Ruben, one of the hosts of the NBC Network "Talknet" radio show, believes that about 50 percent of the couples who come for counseling are able to commit to making changes,[1] and 50 percent are not. (Within the Christian community the commitment rate is probably higher.) In some instances, helping couples uncouple in a healthy manner may be more successful than keeping them together in a destructive relationship.
- Your idea of a good solution to the problem may be different from the ideas of the couple involved.
- You can't make choices for the people involved. Nor can you make them take action.
- You can't fix the marriage or change things in it.
- You can't redo the couple's past.
- You can't be an effective counselor if you are also the client's personal friend.
- You can't be responsible for choices the clients may make.

Most of these limitations are self-explanatory. But let us comment on the importance of not being personal friends with a client. Being a personal friend will no doubt cloud your ability to gain insight into the concerns presented. It may hamper your ability to confront issues. Lastly, the sharing of intimate information may put pressure on the friendship. To be fair to your friend and fair to yourself, it is best to refer a friend to another counselor.

This is probably not an exhaustive list of the limitations. However, it is a good list to think about in order to determine your expectations. The counselor's particular set of values may also result in less effective counseling. For instance, we personally believe that growing up in a healthy two-parent family is the best situation for children. This predisposes us not to face the fact that the best solution may be separation or divorce. Based on our values, we may feel too responsible for making a particular marriage work.

It is not possible or desirable to completely separate your values from the situation. The counselor, however, may reveal his or her values without imposing those values on the counselee. For example, we will share, if appropriate, our belief (value) that many more couples could make their marriages work if they were more committed to doing so. Not all of our couples share this belief.

Let's look at some realistic expectations for the counselor.

- You may be able to help set achievable goals by helping to identify the real issues involved and whose issues they are.
- You may be able to help with behavior changes that will work toward achieving the goals of the couple.
- You may be able to help sort out various options and the consequences of choosing or not choosing these options.
- You can work with the couple as a team to try to find solutions.
- You can help the couple identify strengths and how they might use their strengths in a particular situation.
- You can help individuals develop more control over their own destinies. (By taking responsibility for one's own happiness, greater happiness in the marriage may follow.)
- You may be able to help the couple accept past events. They can learn that the past does not always have to forecast the future.
- You may be able to act as a stabilizing force when the couple has lost hope.

When you are clear about such issues, you will then be able to share realistic expectations for counseling with the clients. You might share these expectations this way:

I've listened to some of your concerns. It will be important to collect some more history and information and to set some goals. I would count it a privilege to work with you in trying to do this. In this sense I'll become a team member with you. But I can't fix your marriage for you. There is no magic in counseling. Counseling is really working together to discover some achievable outcomes for you.

I do not see my role as one of judge and jury. I do see my role as one of helping you explore possible changes and how to accomplish them. This may involve trouble-shooting along the way. Do you have any questions or comments about this? If you do, please state them. That is one of your responsibilities.

Taking the time to do this not only helps give the couple an idea of what to expect realistically but it may also give the feeling of some sense of direction for the next step in the counseling process.

DECISIONS, DIRECTIONS, AND DATA COLLECTION

Standardized Tests

The counselor makes decisions based on data. The data used may be collected formally and systematically by using tests and questionnaires. We also collect data informally by observation. As a rule, the objective procedures are more accurate and less susceptible to counselor bias than the subjective measures. Clinical measures—therapist observations and hunches—are less accurate in describing the present or predicting the future than actuarial measures—standardized tests with good validity and reliability.[2]

The counselor may use standardized tests and reliable rating scales when they are available and if he or she has the appropriate training. If one or both of the above conditions are lacking, the counselor will use less refined data-collection methods. This is not bad. Even the most highly trained, credentialed psychologist will use more informal measures in marriage counseling, simply because standardized instruments do not exist to cover all the issues a couple might face.

We have had training in the use of certain psychological tests. In our practice we might use The Minnesota Multiphasic

Personality Inventory (MMPI),[3] The Millon Clinical Multiaxial Inventory (MCMI),[4] The Myers-Briggs Type Indicator (MBTI),[5] or The Taylor-Johnson Temperament Analysis (TJTA).[6] Training for the MMPI or MCMI requires admission to a doctoral-level training program in psychology. Training for pastors in the MBTI is available if you have had a graduate-level, tests-and-measurements course. Training in the TJTA is available without such prerequisites.

We find these tests (MMPI, MCMI, MBTI, and TJTA) help us understand the psychology and personality of the individual. These tests—especially the MMPI and MCMI—help identify individual psychopathology. Many couples will be free of major psychopathology. If there is any suspicion that one or both of the partners may have a significant psychological problem, it is wise to have a clinical assessment done. We have both worked with couples for a number of sessions and later wished we had given an MMPI or MCMI at the beginning of the counseling relationship.

It is strongly suggested, if you are not trained in using tests like the MMPI, that you establish a consulting relationship with a psychologist skilled in psychodiagnostics. The input from the psychologist along with the test data could be very useful in establishing a treatment plan.

When doing marriage counseling, in addition to tests that focus on the individual, you need instruments that focus on the interaction between husband and wife. Clinical observation or informal data collection plays a major role in defining the issues in a troubled marriage.

Rating Scales, Inventories, and Lists

The data found in rating scales, inventories, and lists is similar to those gleaned from the counseling interviews. These instruments provide a more concise and systematic way to organize the client's data. Since clients may fill them out on their own time, collecting this information doesn't take up interview time. These instruments systematically elicit client's feelings, beliefs, values, interests, problems, desires, and history. All of the instruments described below are available to the pastor or church counselor.

One rating scale, Levels of Marital Commitment, was described in chapter 2. In that section both the data collection (at what levels are the clients) and the counselor's decision (how you treat them based on their levels) were described. You can use the Level of Commitment rating scale not only to plan your initial strategy but, by readministering the rating scale at various intervals, to track counseling progress.

Another widely used rating scale is the Locke-Wallace.[7] It, too, measures where persons believe themselves to be in the marriage. The scale, which can be used at any stage in marriage counseling, has been employed to determine the effectiveness of intervention strategies in many published studies. It measures marital satisfaction in several dimensions. The Locke-Wallace is not commercially distributed. However, a university library should have a copy of the journal article in which the rating scale originally appeared.

One commercially available inventory is the Marital Pre-Counseling Inventory by Richard Stuart and Frieda Stuart.[8] This is a multifaceted instrument which gives a detailed analysis of each couple's strengths and problem areas. This assessment tool can either be hand- or computer-scored. Richard Stuart and Barbara Jacobson have developed a companion marital-therapy tool, *Couple's Therapy Workbook.*[9] The workbook covers the topics of caring behaviors; communication assessment; decision making; division of home, childcare, and work responsibilities; and conflict management. Both of these instruments may be ordered from Research Press, Box 3177, Champaign, Illinois 61821.

Another inventory useful in both premarital and marital counseling is the *Marriage Success Development Inventory* by one of the authors (DeLoss).[10] The MSDI has twenty statements in each of ten areas (two hundred items total). The topic areas are communication, roles, sex and love, religious-social, personality, social relationships, children, in-laws, finances, and activities. In taking the MSDI, clients state how much they agree or disagree with each statement. Next, the client indicates how important that item is to him or her by stating how he or she would feel if the partner were to hold the opposite point of view on that item. The computer print-out highlights areas of agreement (strengths in the marriage) and areas of disagreement on issues identified as important (weaknesses in the marriage). The MSDI also allows the clients to assess how well they know their partners by stating how they think their partners will answer the items. Counselors may obtain information about this instrument by writing MSDI, 6485 Palomino Way, West Linn, Oregon 97068.

Another type of instrument is the life history questionnaire. This can be informal, with a number of categories followed by several blank lines on which to write the answers. Categories could include early childhood, relationship with parents, relationship with siblings, social development, sexual development and experiences, educational history, vocational history, previous marriages, relationship with children, present marriage strengths, and present marriage weaknesses. One of the most widely used commercial instruments of this sort is the Life History Questionnaire by Arnold Lazarus.[11] This is available through Research Press in Champaign, Illinois.

We have included in Appendix 3 a Confidential Data Inventory. While the inventory is lengthy, it can supply you with a great deal of information. You may get some resistance because of its length and apparent intrusiveness. Because of this, we would not recommend its use until after the first counseling session. This will be most beneficial with moderate-to-long-term counseling. We generally do not use this form with couples whom we know are short-term clients.

Another useful tool is the Marital Needs Questionnaire developed by Willard Harley.[12] As we have stated earlier, we believe that one person begins to withdraw need-meeting behavior from the partner when he or she perceives that needs are not being met. When one spouse recognizes what the partner's needs are, and works at meeting those needs, the probability of having his or her own needs met is greatly increased. This questionnaire is useful in helping couples pinpoint their areas of unmet needs. It may be found in his book, *His Needs, Her Needs.*

We have discussed specific assessment tools. It is also important to determine when to begin the assessment. At some point you will want some idea of the couple's history and what the pressing issues in the couple's relationship are.

Couple History

One couple may be ready to focus on history at the start of counseling, while another couple must deal with pressing issues first. It isn't necessary to always start with a couple history.

Most couples have specific issues they want to resolve, and they may be willing to wait before dealing with these issues until the counselor has set some structure for the counseling. If you have indicated in your expectations of counseling that you first want to review the history of the relationship, many couples comply.

There are several reasons for reviewing the history of the couple.

- Often a couple enters counseling with a degree of urgency that can force the counselor into drawing premature conclusions regarding the most effective course of action. Listening to a detailed history gives you a better perspective, more accurate data, and reduces the pressure for immediate action.
- Listening to a chronology of the relationship allows the counselor to see the issues that occur repeatedly. It is more fruitful to resolve dysfunctional behavior that occurs repeatedly than to focus on rare dysfunctional behavior (unless the behavior is of crisis proportions, e.g., spouse abuse).
- You can mentally assess the prognosis of this relationship and look for strengths on which to build your interventions. One thing you look for is evidence of earlier love or happiness. If this has occurred in the past there is good reason love or happiness can develop again. With positive elements in their history, couples can be encouraged that there is hope for future happiness.
- It is important to collect the marital history with both people present. It is not unusual for the more dissatisfied spouse to distort history. Whether the distortion is causing the unhappiness or the unhappiness is causing the distortion is immaterial.

We are familiar with a troubled couple in their late thirties. The husband, who was questioning staying in the marriage, raised questions about the selection of the furniture they owned. "Even the furniture reflects your tastes and personality," he told his wife. "What furniture would you have if you had your way?" she asked. "Oriental modern," he answered. She thought a moment, and then said, "When we got married, the kind of furniture I liked was French Provincial. We compromised and purchased Italian Provincial. Our furniture represents a blend of what would have been our individual first choices." "I'd forgotten that. I guess you're right," he said.

It is so easy to recast history in a way that justifies the dissatisfied partner's complaints. Having both people present can help keep the record straight.

Part of the purpose of history taking is to identify the strengths of the couple. And one way to do that is to identify what attracted each to the other in the first place. Secondly, you may wish to have them summarize their strengths by asking what they believe is working for them.

Determining pressing issues. We want to know what the couple sees as their most pressing issues. If you started with the history, you may now see a number of areas on which to place the focus of counseling. However, it is best to wait for the couple to identify their areas of concern. Something that seems like a pressing issue to you may be of minor importance to your counselees.

At the close of the first session, we often assign the task of writing down all the issues each partner wants addressed in counseling. These can include behaviors the partners want to see stopped or decreased, and/or started or increased.

After they have written down their issues of concern we ask them to prioritize the lists. If there are a number of related items, we find it useful to group them. We may end up with several categories (e.g., in-laws, disciplining of children, finances), each with two or three specific items. This makes a long list of complaints more manageable, and they thus appear more resolvable to the clients.

The issues on which you will get the most cooperation are those that both spouses have rated of high priority. It is best to start with these. The only time we temporarily bypass a category of high priority is when the high-priority issue is very difficult to resolve and a lower (but important) issue would be comparatively easy. Getting some early positive results has a motivating effect.

Paul Hauck, in his book *Three Faces of Love,* suggests that each partner ask three questions:[13]

1. What are my deepest desires and needs? Not to own a Rolls Royce or be a U.S. senator, but what truly are the most important things in a relationship for me?
2. What are my partner's abilities, aptitudes, and traits? Can my partner meet my deepest desires and needs?
3. Is my partner willing to meet my needs if he or she is able?

If a person's deepest desires and needs are specified, and if the partner is able and willing to meet them, then the prognosis is excellent. If, on the other hand, the partner is able but unwilling to meet these needs, you will need to help negotiate either a change in willingness or a change in needs before work on the marriage itself can begin.

Charting the Course

Setting goals is like charting a course. A couple can determine the ultimate destination and then break the trip down into workable, definable segments. The goals may be accomplished in one session or may take much longer.

For example, a newly married couple may be seeking some information on how they can develop a budget. They want materials they can read and forms they can use. When this is accomplished, the goal is achieved. The counselor may wish to invite them back after a period of time to see how things are going.

On the other hand, and most often, the goals are not easily defined and established. It may take several sessions of data collection before you can establish definable behavioral goals. In part, this may be because the counselor needs to work with the couple to help them define the problem area or underlying cause. You, the counselor, can summarize what you hear the couple establishing as the problem area(s) and what they would like to change.

If possible, it is desirable to establish measurable behaviors based on the couple's desires and the counselor's expertise (i.e., increased couple time together or practicing clarifying exercises). We might diagram the process like this.

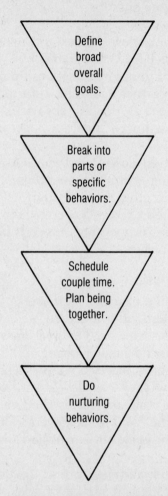

Fig. 5.1   Behavior Flowchart

Some intermediary individual steps may be integrated into the flow chart. For example, an individual may need to deal with anger or fear that has built up over time.

Goal setting may be viewed as part of a long process. Once

one goal is achieved, another may be set and the subsequent goal may depend upon how the previous goal was met. It is constructive to summarize and establish agreement with the couple when establishing the goals. This agreement becomes a part of the process. Thus, the process of setting goals with the couple will help them look at the broad picture as well as at smaller, definable, workable segments. Both perspectives will help lead toward the achievement of the broad goal.

WHEN TO WORK INDIVIDUALLY WHILE DOING COUPLE THERAPY

Earlier, we discussed whether it is ever appropriate to see one of the partners individually. We are assuming that it is. Since we have previously addressed the "if," we will now address the "when." Deciding to work individually does not undermine the underlying goal of helping the couple move toward being able to work together. Rather, it augments the couple's work. The time spent in individual work may be as short as five minutes or as long as several sessions.

The following are some situations in which working with the individual may be the preferred choice.

- When the partners are at extremely different levels of commitment, but do not wish to leave the relationship. Often, it is very important to meet with the spouses individually in order to sort out the options and the consequences of those options. For example, the spouse who wants to leave the relationship has the power and, if the other partner pushes for a decision, that partner is apt to hear what he or she does not wish to hear. Allowing nonpressured time for the partner to do additional sorting is very important. The partner desiring the relationship needs to know this.
- Educating or sharing of information needs to be done privately. For example, some partners have not learned to do nurturing behaviors automatically. They don't even think about doing nurturing behaviors. It's not that they don't wish to do them, they just don't think about them. Privately, you can encourage the use of reminders such as—making a note in an appointment book as a reminder to do something

for the spouse or writing down thoughts that occurred during the day that can be shared with the partner.

- When one partner overpowers the other so much you can't collect data or establish rapport with the other partner. Individual sessions may be necessary to establish trust with that partner.
- When the couple's interactions are so volatile, you can't make any headway. You may need to do individual work to deal with anger.
- When you have a "romantic" idealist who says it doesn't count if someone has to tell you or if "I have to ask" for certain behaviors. You may wish to deal with the romantic individual privately to shape more realistic expectations. At the same time, you may wish to work with the other partner to develop more nurturing behaviors. If this is done privately, the resulting, nurturing behaviors will not be so apt to be discounted by the romantic.

ACCENTUATE THE POSITIVE, ELIMINATE THE NEGATIVE

In its most simple form, a happy marriage has a high percentage of positive interactions and characteristics and a low percentage of negative ones. Conversely, an unhappy marriage has a surplus of negatives and a deficit of positive interactions. Thinking of the issues in terms of positives and negatives gives you some additional criteria for structuring your counseling goals.

While the ultimate goal is to build up the positives, that is not always the place to start. If a couple resists your attempts to introduce positive experiences you might make more headway by focusing on eliminating the negative. Kari and Warren seemed to delight in finding each other's flaws. Each put the other down with regularity. Although each did it to the other, each one hated it when it was done to him or her. It is also true that Kari and Warren spent little time in enjoyable activities together.

Encouraging this couple to spend more time together could prove futile if the level of hostility is very high. Even pleasurable events can become negative. It is more important to help this couple learn to handle hostility first. Once that is accomplished, future events are more likely to be positive.

Where there are many negative issues, you may find yourself working at eliminating the negatives for a long time before the couple is willing to plan for positive events.

Brush Fires and Forest Fires

We define brush fires as those day-to-day problems that crop up in everyone's life. Individually, a brush fire is minor. Because there are so many of them, however, they can be important. A forest fire, on the other hand, is a major, or *the* major issue in the relationship. Most often a couple comes to counseling because of a forest fire in the marriage.

The first counseling session with Tami and Pete appeared successful. Several major problems were described and both agreed concerning the importance of the problems. The most major concern was Pete's overinvolvement with his family. Tami felt that his parents had gained a new daughter but after two years of marriage she didn't feel she had gained a husband.

By the end of the third session, the topics discussed were Pete's recent performance review at work, a crisis with Tami's sister, the joys and traumas of a new puppy, and Pete's not calling when he was going to be late.

These were all important to the couple, but if this trend continued, it would be easy for Pete and Tami to conclude they weren't getting anywhere in counseling. Why? Because their major problem was still there.

We know the brush fires are real and are important. They happen to all of us. They are the stuff out of which life is made. But if that is all the counselor focuses upon, there will be little or no time left for the forest fires.

We usually don't deal openly with this unless it becomes a concern. In many counseling situations the couple deals with the brush fires of life for a while and then moves to the forest fire. When this doesn't happen, the counselor will want to ask which direction they wish to go—brush fires or forest fires?

Tami and Pete, I noticed during our second and third counseling session that we never came back to the primary concern we discussed during our first session. That was Pete's ties to his family. I know we've talked about important things, but I'm afraid that if we continue this way, after a while you will feel that we are not addressing the crucial issue. What I'd like to suggest is that we spend the first half of each session talking about whatever is going on in your lives that would be important to evaluate here. But when the first half-hour is gone, let's change the focus to Pete's relationship to his family. Does that make some sense?

Of course, this approach need not be rigidly enforced. But as a principle, it will enhance movement in the more crucial areas. The couple will thus give time to define and redefine what the forest fires are for them.

Contracting and Accountability

In order to avoid floundering and moving on a chartless course, it is important to determine some specific tasks appropriate to the stage of counseling. These tasks may be specific homework assignments. In the early stage, this may consist of having each partner list certain behaviors that would make one feel special. (You need to define what is meant by "behaviors.") They are then to rank these in order of importance. You, the counselor, contract with each partner that they will do one or more of these items for the partner by the next session. They will bring their lists in hand. They will be responsible and accountable to you. This is reinforced if you write the assignment out as a prescription and give it to them. It is even more powerful if it is written as a contract and signed by the counselees.

There are at least two benefits to this process. The person gains a sense of action, of finally doing something. And you, the counselor, now have a tool for measuring compliance. Did the individual do what was agreed? If not, why not? The answers may help you determine the next step.

Summary

The intent of this chapter has been to provide a framework in which the counselor can plan the most effective course of action. It is very important at the beginning to establish realistic expectations. This starts with the counselor setting reachable personal goals. It is then important to determine the counselee's expectations and confirm or correct them.

Once the general direction is determined, you may collect necessary data through counselee self-report, assessment inventories, and psychological tests. Then, by understanding your limitations, knowing the person's expectations and having relevant data available, you can define the goals of counseling for a specific couple. Part of your treatment plan may include some individual work. When this is done, the focus is on the couple.

Sometimes you will find that more headway is made by working on increasing the positive elements in the marriage. At other times, any attempt to be positive is resisted. When this happens, the option is to work on the elimination of negative aspects.

Even though you have set reasonable and acceptable goals, you may find the counselees focusing on what happened last week rather than on their stated goals. A method for working both with the day-to-day issues—brush fires—and the long term issues—forest fires—was discussed.

Finally, ideas for contracting and other ways to improve client accountability were presented.

CHAPTER SIX

THE MARITAL PYRAMID AND THE PLACE OF COMMUNICATION

The marital pyramid illustrates well the importance of an integrated approach to marriage counseling. While the upper levels of the pyramid relate to the interaction of the couple, the bottom layer relates mainly to the health of the individual.

The marital pyramid has four layers. The bottom or foundation layer is *individual emotional health*. Individual emotional or mental health has a great bearing on the health of the marriage. No one has perfect emotional responses and attitudes. However, it is important to a successful marriage for both partners to be free of any major emotional or mental problems.

Any major psychiatric disorder—depression, anxiety, phobia, manic-depressive (bipolar) illness, schizophrenia, or paranoia—

56

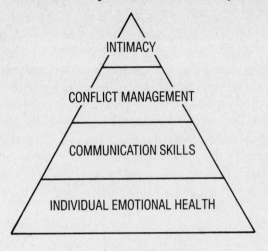

Fig. 6.1 The Marital Pyramid

and any significant personality disorder—asocial, avoidant, antisocial, dependent, histrionic, narcissistic, passive-aggressive, or borderline—can contaminate the higher levels of the marital pyramid. (Please refer to chapter 5 for a description of personality tests helpful in diagnosing psychopathology.)

These psychiatric disorders, when found in your clients, do not have to be completely eliminated before moving ahead in marriage counseling. If the problems are reduced to manageable levels you can proceed. For example, before individual therapy, an overly dependent husband was always labeling his wife's activities with her friends as selfish and inconsiderate of his feelings. After therapy, he still sometimes felt the same way but recognized the cause being his strong need for security and reassurance, rather than her being selfish.

The importance of sometimes needing to postpone marriage counseling until individual issues are resolved is discussed in chapter 3. We often find that the reason we are not making progress in counseling the marriage is because some individual psychological problems were overlooked.

When you are comfortable with the emotional health of the partners it is time to focus on the *communication skills* of the couple (see Figure 6.1). Some couples state from the beginning of counseling that they want help with their communication. In this case, your plan of what to work on next and the couple's desire is the same. No problem! Your goals match. In more cases, however, the couple will present you with a list of complaints or problems, issues that may be scattered among the upper three levels of the pyramid. It is appropriate for you to give them opportunity to describe why they have come to you. After you have given them a chance to express themselves, and you have an understanding of their situation, it is time to switch focus. You will now want to explain the importance of developing good communication skills before attempting to resolve some of their more pressing problems.

When communication skills are reasonably well developed you can now address their methods of *conflict management.* Learning to problem solve and manage conflict proceeds more smoothly than if you had attempted this task without first acquiring good communication skills.

Intimacy is at the top of the pyramid (again, you may wish to refer to Figure 6.1). It is the hallmark of a good marriage. Trying to help the couple achieve intimacy when there are major unresolved conflict issues is not likely to work. This does not mean the couple has to be completely conflict-free, but that conflict is at an acceptable level to the couple before proceeding with intimacy issues.

This chapter on communication, and the ones that follow on conflict management and intimacy, use the marital pyramid. All of the issues a marriage counselor confronts do not fit nicely into the pyramid structure. However, the concept of dealing with lower-level issues before moving to higher-level ones should prove helpful.

We find the pyramid useful to guide our thinking about the marriage counseling process. The marital pyramid may be even more helpful to show to couples. They can better understand the necessity of dealing with lower-level concerns before working with higher-level ones.

COMMUNICATION

By this time in the counseling process, a counseling relationship has been formed, some assessment has been made, and any major individual psychopathology is being treated. Even though the couple cites conflict as the major problem, it is necessary that you examine their communication skills.

Bornstein and Bornstein[1] report that as many as 90 percent of all distressed couples cite communication difficulties as a major problem in their relationships. Communication may not be the most important area with a specific couple, but it is the first one you encounter. For example, a couple comes to you with conflicts about who is responsible for what task around the house. You work with them on resolving the role conflicts. However the couple keeps getting bogged down by their misunderstanding of each other. The counselor may say:

I know, Martha, that you are really frustrated with Bill regarding the sharing of jobs around the house, and you'd like us to tackle that problem first. We've discussed the issue for some time and seem to be stuck. I'd like to temporarily change focus. I think you both would benefit from learning how to communicate clearly without misunderstanding. I believe the first step in solving a problem is often learning how to talk about the problem. If this is agreeable, let's work on some basic communication skills now.

We communicate to each other in a variety of ways. Speaking to one another—verbal communication—is our main way of sending messages. In addition, many messages are sent nonverbally. Let's look at nonverbal communication first.

NONVERBAL COMMUNICATION

Human beings communicate not only with words but with the body as well. Julian Fast in *Body Language* describes in detail the various messages that are sent and received with one's body.[2] Warren and Warren describe five aspects of body language relevant to marital communication: eye contact, facial expression, posture, gestures, and voice characteristics.[3]

Eye Contact. Looking at the other person, both when speaking and listening, implies that what is being said is important. This is not crucial in casual conversation (nor safe when one is driving a car). Trying to read the newspaper, keeping one eye

59

on the television or making sure you don't drop a knitting stitch communicates to the other person that the project at hand is more important than the subject being discussed. Many people can do two things at once but there are times when it is best to set aside the distractions and give each other full attention.

Facial Expression. Frowning, puffing out one's cheeks, rolling the eyes, or pursing the lips often communicates anger, disbelief, or disapproval. These are communication stoppers. A pleasant or at least neutral facial expression will communicate that the message is being heard.

Posture. Facing and turning your body toward the other communicates receptivity. Assuming an open body position, arms at the side, also communicates receptivity. If you sit or stand with arms folded across your chest with your body turned away from the other person staring off into space, your nonverbal cues will often be interpreted as being nonreceptive or even defensive.

Gestures. Some of the common negative gestures are pointing one's finger (you did wrong), shrugs of the shoulders (I don't care), or shaking one's head no (you are wrong). Positive gestures include the absence of negative gestures, plus nodding one's head up and down (I hear you) or leaning toward the other (this is important).

Voice Characteristics. Negative traits are accusing tones, loud volume, or whining. "A soft answer turneth away wrath" (Prov. 15:1 KJV) is the classic example of positive voice characteristics.

Semiverbal. These are more nonverbal than verbal, but they are heard by the other person. Heavy sighs or the blowing of air are examples that are usually interpreted negatively.

Overt Behaviors. Slamming doors, banging drawers, throwing things around, and careless or fast driving are usually perceived as outbursts of anger. Many of the negative nonverbal cues are perceived as anger. While it is common to feel anger during a discussion of sensitive issues, it is usually an impediment to communication to display the anger. Anger in one person usually begets anger in the other person.

The negative nonverbal cues are labeled negative because that is usually how they are read by others. That does not mean, however, that the negatively interpreted cue was intended negatively. The person with arms folded across the chest is often interpreted as being closed or defensive. Could it be that this person is merely cold (body temperature) and is trying to keep warm? Is it even possible to spin the wheels on the gravel accidentally? Or is every occurrence of this a sign of an angry, impatient person? In later sections we will deal with the importance of checking out what the other means by both verbal and nonverbal messages.

Gross physical behaviors, such as pointing a finger or throwing up one's arms, are easy to identify. If a spouse says, "Please don't point your finger at me as if I were a naughty child," there will be little disagreement as to whether the finger was pointed. However, if one says, "Please don't shout at me," a response of "I'm not shouting!" is frequently heard. The level of intensity at which a behavior becomes objectionable will vary with the person.

The use of a tape recorder can identify whether the perceived tone of voice was as harsh as it sounded to the listener. Playing back the tape can be revealing. Sometimes the listener, who believed the partner to be shouting, is surprised to find that his or her voice doesn't sound that loud on the playback. Or, the speaker is surprised to hear how loud he or she really became. Awareness must precede changes in behavior or perception.

Facial cues can often be tracked by having the couple prop up a mirror on a table and discuss a matter in full view of the mirror. By monitoring one's own facial expressions, seeing ourselves as others see us, it is easier to become aware and to control those expressions. This awareness is useful because often a person gives external signs of anger before he or she is fully aware of the internal feelings of anger.

VERBAL COMMUNICATION

Blaming

Many counselees come into counseling with a blaming communication style. As a result the partner responds in a defensive manner. Jerome told us:

Jane asks me to do one thing with our son and before I'm really into doing that she's telling me I should be spending more time with our daughter. I'm tired after working hard all day. After a while, I just throw up my hands and go to sleep on the sofa.

(Internally he is saying, "I can't stand this one more time. She's never going to get off my back. She plays all day going to her women's meetings and expects me to help pick up the pieces.")

The technique of using "I" messages helps the individual move from the nonproductive blaming to a sharing of genuine feelings and what may be producing those feelings. The person begins with identifying what emotion is felt and follows with constructive information connected to the feelings. Someone may say, "I feel overwhelmed and that turns to anger when I'm trying to do what I think you have asked—only to be told what else I should be doing. I feel like I'll never please you and this will never end."

"I" messages can help defuse the anger and move the conversation to a level where some change can be decided upon.

Shirts and Garbage Cans

Trying to discuss more than one issue at a time adds communication clutter for many couples. Let's look at a case study. Marie and David had settled into a pattern: she would see that his work shirts would be in the closet, ready to go when he needed them, and David assumed responsibility for seeing that the kitchen trash was taken out to the garbage cans. They had no formal agreement that one kind of work was contingent upon the other.

One morning David went to the closet and found no work shirts. "Marie," he called, "I don't have any work shirts." Marie, feeling guilty, called back, "You haven't taken care of the kitchen trash this week either."

They are now talking about two different topics. Both David and Marie had not done their chores. Conflict can most readily be resolved by dealing with one issue at a time. When couples can think in terms of dealing first with one topic (shirts) and then moving to the next topic (garbage), they can make more progress toward resolution. David said, "I don't have any clean work shirts." How different it might have been had Marie responded: "I'm sorry. I had them set out to iron yesterday and I got sidetracked. I'll do one right away. Oh, by the way, I'd appreciate your checking the kitchen trash."

COMMUNICATION MODELS

Intent-Impact Model

The writers of *A Couple's Guide to Communication* found in their research on distressed versus nondistressed couples that there was no difference between the two groups regarding the original intent of a message.[4] A partner in a distressed marriage was just as likely to have a positive intent behind what was first said in a verbal interaction as the speaker in a nondistressed marriage. However, the spouse in the distressed marriage was much more likely to interpret the remark as negative than was a nondistressed listener.

In *A Couple's Guide to Communication,* Figure 6.2 is presented to describe the Intent-Impact Communication model. In that model the *intent* person is the speaker and the *impact* person is the listener. If communication were perfect (we would call it heavenly communication) the impact of the message would be exactly the same as the intent. We would know exactly

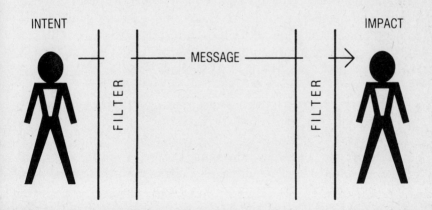

Fig. 6.2   Intent-Impact Communication Model—Phase I

what the other person meant. Every nuance of thought, all of the necessary background information, would be presented. No miscommunication would occur.

Earthly communication is not perfect. The diagram shows us why. The speaker speaks through a filter and the listener listens through another filter. The message passes through two filters. If the filters are clear (or nearly so) the message passes through unaltered. The impact is the same as the intention. When the filters are clouded, the message gets distorted. The greater the cloudiness the greater the distortion.

Filters can become clouded for several reasons. If a person is tired, ill, pressed for time, suffering from a physical ailment, or is under stress, words can be said that were not intended and heard that were not implied.

More potent conditions may cloud the filter as well. A person's family background can influence filtering. The person raised in a family that uses a lot of sarcasm can innocently say something that sounds like a put-down to someone who grew up in a very polite family.

Previous relationships can clog the filter, also. The wife in a remarriage may find her filter filling with suspicion when her husband says he is too tired to make love. Perhaps her first husband said this when he was having an affair.

The couple's own relationship-history is often the biggest problem in the filter. Most people have been hurt or let down by their partners at some time. Distressed couples have experienced hurt many times and this past history affects the filter. It is very easy to interpret what is presently being said in light of what has gone on in the past. If we have ever had the thought, *there he goes again,* or *that may not have been what you said, but I know what you meant,* we were using a filter clouded with past history.

Remember the previously cited research. Communicators in distressed marriages have the same degree of positive intent as those in nondistressed marriages. Listeners in distressed marriages are much more likely to interpret the message as negative. This is not to say that all the problems in distressed marriages lie with the listener. Nor does this research say that only one of the distressed partners misinterprets. In distressed marriages, each partner, when it is his or her turn to be the receiver of the message, is likely to respond negatively.

Penni and Al have had conflicts regarding her family. Al believes he has come to terms with her family and realizes that spending time with them is important to Penni. For the last few years, they have spent the Easter weekends with them. About six weeks before Easter, Al and Penni are discussing the events of the day. Al says, "I've got a great idea for Easter this year."

What do you think Penni's response is? It most likely depends on whether they are a distressed or nondistressed couple. If they are a nondistressed couple, Penni and Al's interaction might go something like this.

Al: I've got a great idea for Easter this year!

Penni: (*Al knows I like to spend Easter with my parents so I bet he has something special.*) "Oh, really! What do you have in mind?

Al: You know Easter is early this year and the snow is still good. Bob, at work, has a timeshare at Sunriver that week but they have to leave early for a wedding. We can have Friday and Saturday night for only $50 rather than the $250 those condos usually rent for. There is even enough room for your family if you would like to do that.

Now consider this same plan, but this time, the couple is distressed.

Al: I've got a great idea for Easter this year!

Penni: (*There he goes again, trying to get out of being with my parents. He thinks his parents are so wonderful. He makes me sick!*). Does Al's Mommy want her little boy to hunt for Easter eggs at her house?

Al: (*Forget trying to do anything nice. It makes me so mad the way she always attacks my Mom.*) Matter of fact, spending Easter with my family is a lot more pleasant than the garbage I have to put up with around your family.

As we compare the dialogue of the nondistressed Al and Penni with the distressed Al and Penni several concepts are illustrated. First, the original intent of the two Als was the same—positive. Second, the impact on Penni (how she perceived Al's words) was different. The nondistressed Penni did not have any recent negative history in her filter concerning Al not liking her parents. The distressed Penni did. Third, even though the distressed Al had a positive intent, see how quickly he moved to a negative response. He has some recent negative history in his filter regarding Penni's feelings about his mother.

If Al had been truly nondistressed, the interchange, in spite of Penni's negative reaction, might have gone like this:

Al: *(Penni thinks I still don't like her parents. Some things die hard, I guess. I want to reassure her that was not my intent.)* Penni, what I had in mind had nothing to do with my mother or any intent at avoiding your family. (And then he goes on to describe Bob's offer and how they might use it.)

When communication breaks down, both parties have a responsibility to clarify their meaning. While the listener (the impact person) has the first responsibility to seek clarification, the speaker also has responsibility. First, the speaker has the responsibility to state the message in such a way, with positive nonverbal cues, that is likely to be well received by the listener. Second, if it is clear to the speaker that the listener misunderstood the message then, as seen in the last example, clarification is in order.

The Intent-Impact model is often called the three-way communication model. The first part is the original message. The second part is the listener's response to the impact. The second part will be discussed next.

Phase II in the figure labels the listener's response as Check-Out. When the impact is negative the listener has the responsibility to check out the true meaning of the speaker's message. We share the following principles with our clients:

When you experience a negative reaction (negative impact) to what your partner said, that impact was not caused

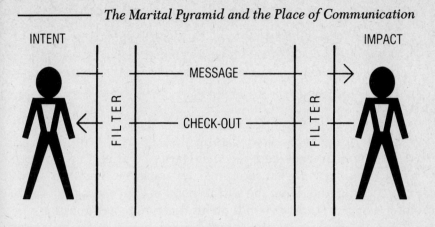

Fig. 6.3 Intent-Impact Communication Model—Phase II

totally by your partner's words. They did not produce your feeling. Instead, your partner's words, as interpreted by you, produced your feelings. The stuff in your filter caused your interpretation. A better emotional equation is:

your partner's words × your interpretation = your feelings.

In mathematics $2 \times 3 = 6$. Making an alteration in one factor changes the end result. Similarly, if you change your perception, the second factor in the emotional equation, your feelings will change also. How do you know your perception is right or wrong?

Everyone is affected by what is said. Everyone has perceptions. If you view your perception as a guess concerning your partner's meaning, rather than as an absolute fact, you will be ready to check out your partner. Your way to check will be a question to clarify your partner's intent. You will ask your question in a nonjudgmental, nonaccusing manner. Let's see how Penni could have used these concepts in her response to Al.

Al: I've got a great idea for Easter this year!"

Penni: (*Oh, there he goes again. Trying to get out of being with my family. Now wait a minute. That is only a guess on my part. I know he used to do that and maybe he is doing that again. I don't know. I'd better find out what he means.*) I'd like to clarify something I'm thinking. Are you saying you don't want to be with my family on Easter?

Penni has put her suspicion on hold. She is on the verge of being hurt and angry as she has been in the past. With training in the Intent-Impact model she has learned that her feelings are often a product of what she thinks was meant rather than what was actually said. How she will respond in the remainder of the interchange with Al depends on his reaction to her question.

The third phase of the Intent-Impact model is the original speaker's response to the Check-Out. When Al was questioned as to whether he was saying he didn't want to spend Easter with Penni's parents, he had two basic response options: confirm Penni's suspicions or correct them. Confirm or correct is the label of the third part in the three-way communication model.

If Al's intention had been that he didn't like Penni's family and that he never wanted to spend another Easter with them, he would confirm her first interpretation. There would be bad feelings, but there would be no miscommunication. The intent and the impact would be the same. This would be genuine conflict. Al's intention, however, was positive. His answer to Penni's check-out would be to correct the initial interpretation.

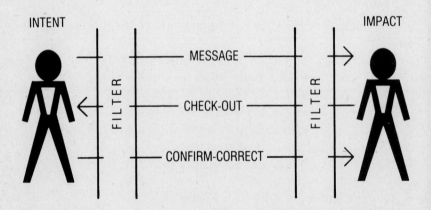

Fig. 6.4   Intent-Impact Communication Model—Phase III

Al: Oh no! That isn't it at all. (And then he goes on to describe Bob's offer and his plan.)

The importance of believing the correction must be emphasized. People often believe the worst in order to prevent a later surprise. It seems as though humans, once they've been hurt, prefer to believe the worst and be wrong than to believe the best and be wrong. We find that most couples tell each other the truth in this three-way communication model. If Al tells the truth nine out of ten times, is it more to Penni's advantage to always believe him when she checks him out? Of course it is. She will have a 90-percent success rate. If she never believes him, she is protecting herself from unpleasant surprises but she is wrong 90 percent of the time. It is better, unless one is married to a psychopathic liar, to give the other the benefit of the doubt.

Transactional Analysis Model

The Transactional Analysis, or TA, model overlaps very nicely with the Intent-Impact model. Although many of the same issues are covered, some couples seem to identify more with one model than with another.

The TA approach was first presented by Eric Berne in his book *Games People Play.* Later, a more popular treatment of TA was given in *I'm O.K., You're O.K.* by William Harris. As a comprehensive psychotherapy approach, TA has its shortcomings. However, as a communication model we find it very effective.

According to TA, there are three different components to a personality: Parent, Adult, and Child. The Child is the first part of the personality to develop, and contains our feelings and desires. A baby is a bundle of feelings and desires. If a baby gets what he or she desires, happiness is the result. As we mature we retain our Child; we still have desires and feelings. The Child is also the source of spontaneity, creativity, and the ability to play and have fun. People who are not able to play or who seem to lack feelings are considered to have an underdeveloped Child.

The Adult is the next part of us to develop. The Adult is the problem solver and decision maker, and figures out things. Since the Adult works with facts, he or she is more concerned with whether something will work than if it is right or wrong. The Adult is expedient and pragmatic. It is noncritical and non-judgmental.

The Parent, the third part, has two aspects: critical Parent and nurturing Parent. The critical Parent has the right-wrong judgmental dimension, much like the justice attribute of God. The nurturing Parent is the compassionate part of the personality, much like the mercy attribute of God. One problem with the Parent is that the rules ingrained in the Parent may not be based on fact. They may be too harsh, rigid, unrealistic, and perfectionistic. A similar problem is that some people have mainly a critical Parent with little of a nurturing Parent. Even though the Parent can have excesses, it is very necessary to the personality.

In using TA as a communication model we see the Parent, Adult, and Child from one person interact with the Parent, Adult, and Child of the other person. Even though we

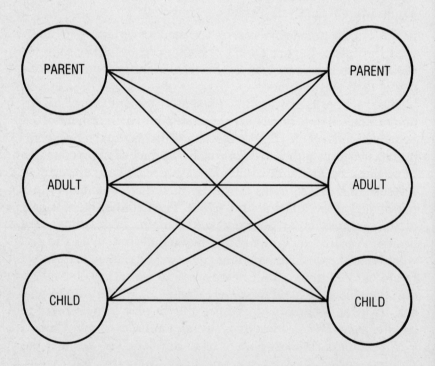

Fig. 6.5 Transactional Analysis Communication Model

have three parts to our personality only one of these parts can communicate to one of the other parts at a time.

In theory, any one part of our personality can communicate to any one part of another's personality. In practice there are two transaction types: horizontal and diagonal. The horizontal transactions (Child to Child, Adult to Adult, and Parent to Parent) usually result in good communication because both people are at the same level—they are equals. The Adult-Adult transaction is where most of the problem solving, data sharing and analyzing, and decision making is done. The diagonal transaction, especially when the people are teenagers or older, is usually problematic.

In using TA to analyze marital communication, we focus on the two troublesome diagonal transactions, Parent-Child and Child-Parent and their healthy alternative, the horizontal Adult-Adult transaction.

Parent to Child. The Parent is in the superior position. The Parent in the critical mode is right. The Child is in the inferior position and is wrong. When we are little, that is acceptable or even desirable. We are ignorant, unskilled, and impulsive. As children we allow our parents to tell us what to do and whether we are right or wrong. As we grow older we begin to resent being treated like children. The heavy-handed parent is the one most likely to experience rebellion coming from his children. Young children accept the absolute authority of the parent. As adults we accept the authority of people we believe are entitled to it, such as law officers, judges, or bosses. We reject the authority of people we believe are not entitled. We become rebellious. In the marital interaction parent-to-child communication is usually critical and judgmental, "I'm right and you are wrong. You must do it my way."

Child to Parent. The Child in us perceives the other as being in the Parent: critical, judgmental, and demanding. That makes us angry and rebellious. "Go fly a kite! I won't listen to you. You are not my boss."

Adult to Adult. In this interaction neither sees the other as critical, judgmental, or rebellious. Requests are made instead of demands. The tone is friendly. Each allows the other his or her point of view. Neither has to have his or her way.

Let's now examine the communication between Ted and Phyllis. The couple stayed up late on Friday night to watch old movies. They agreed since they did not get to bed until after midnight, to sleep in Saturday morning. At a quarter 'til six, their usual rising time, Phyllis's eyes popped open. Discovering that she couldn't get back to sleep, she tried to slip out of bed. However, Ted woke up.

Ted: I thought we were going to sleep in this morning.

Phyllis: I can't get back to sleep. I think I'll go clean out the downstairs bedroom. It needs to be done before our house guests come next month anyway.

Ted: Do you want me to help?

Phyllis: Oh no. We agreed to sleep in. I would if I could.

Ted: When are you going to be through?

Phyllis: I really want to give it a thorough cleaning. About nine o'clock, I guess.

Ted: Well, I'll have a nice breakfast for you at nine.

At about nine o'clock Phyllis comes upstairs where the master bedroom and kitchen are located.

Phyllis: What's for breakfast?

Ted: (Sitting bolt upright in bed, feeling guilty and amazed it is nine o'clock.) "If you want it so bad, why don't you fix it yourself."

Phyllis: (*That rascal. I work three hours while he sleeps and then he insults me when I ask a simple question.*) I might as well. I do all the rest of the work around here.

Ted and Phyllis are off and running on a Saturday-morning fight that could spoil their entire weekend. A TA analysis would show the following:

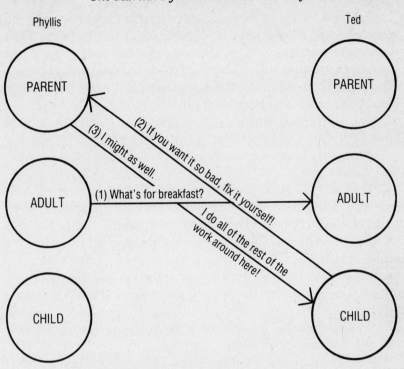

Fig. 6.6   Phyllis and Ted TA Diagram

The diagram shows that Phyllis's first remark (1) was Adult to Adult. However, when Ted awoke, what was his original feeling? Guilt. Whenever we are experiencing feeling we are in our Child. Phyllis was speaking from her Adult but Ted was in his Child. He experienced her comments as coming from her Parent even though they weren't.

Ted's response (2) was directed at who he thought sent the message. It traveled from his rebellious Child to her critical Parent. Phyllis, having just encountered Ted's rebellion, jumped to her critical Parent (3) and fired one off to Ted's Child. She'll show him.

Our counselees are usually laughing at this point because they recognize the interaction. They have done it many times themselves.

While it is useful to show a communication model people can identify with, it must also be one they can use to break their destructive pattern.

Who was responsible (notice the choice of the word *responsible* rather than *fault*) in the interaction between Phyllis and Ted? Both were, Ted first, then Phyllis.

Just like in the Intent-Impact model, these questions need to be asked: What did the other person mean by that? Was she being critical? Is my sensitivity reading in something that really isn't there?

If Ted, after hearing Phyllis's question (1), had asked, "Is that an honest question or did you know I just woke up and you were jabbing me?" Phyllis might have responded, "Ted, I didn't know until right now that you have been asleep all this time. No problem. I wasn't being critical. Do you want me to help fix breakfast or should we go out this morning?" If Ted had only asked the clarifying question (checked-out Phyllis's intent) the fight and the spoiled weekend would have been avoided. Diagrammed in the TA manner, the interchange would look like the diagram on the following page.

We said earlier that Phyllis also had a responsibility to short-circuit the miscommunication. TA is like having a telephone with three lines: Parent, Adult, and Child. We are calling someone who also has three lines: Parent, Adult and Child. We've all dialed a wrong number. We get a response we didn't expect and say, "Oh, I'm sorry, I must have misdialed." Then we try again. We'll replay the interaction between Phyllis and Ted. This time Phyllis will be alert to a wrong number.

Phyllis: What's for breakfast?

Ted: (You know his thoughts already.) If you want it so badly, why don't you fix it yourself?

Phyllis: (*Oh, Oh! Ted's in bed and he is feeling guilty. He fell back to sleep and has just awakened. He thinks I'm on his case. Well, he is a bit of a stinker right now, but it was my Adult, not my Parent speaking. I'll try to reassure him.*) Honey, I hear you are still in bed. No problem. I wasn't

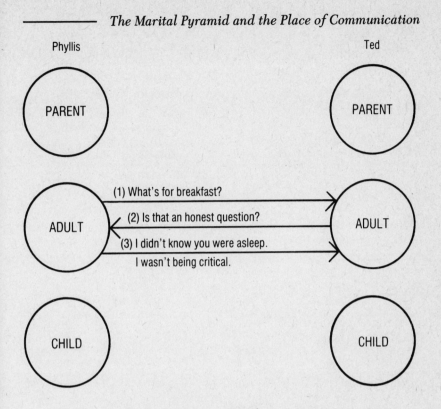

Fig. 6.7   A Second Phyllis and Ted TA Diagram

being smart. Do you want me to help you with breakfast or do you want to eat out?

Ted: I'm sorry. I thought you were sticking it to me for sleeping in. I really had planned to make breakfast. I had no idea I would sleep until nine o'clock.

Remember the concept of the wrong number. When you get a wrong number you hang up and try again. The same thing occurs in marital communication. When we get a response we didn't expect, we can say "wrong number." A different part of the personality picked up the phone. We need to hang up and redial.

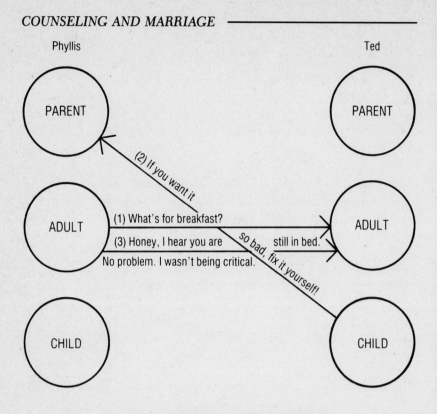

Fig. 6.8   A Third Phyllis and Ted TA Diagram

When both people are responsible for their own feelings (It is what I'm telling myself about what my partner said, more than the words he or she actually said that creates the problem) then communication can truly proceed smoothly.

While one can reach diminishing returns, more communication models can be better. We have constructed a model which, while having a different emphasis, is still consistent with the other two models we find useful.

1-2-3 Communication Model

1-2-3 and A, B, C should be something everyone can remember. We use the 1-2-3 label because it is simple.

1. Feelings are facts. What I feel is what I feel. If I'm feeling scared, I'm scared. If I feel angry, I'm angry. This is the identification and labeling of the emotion being expressed.

2. *Feelings come from a logical thinking process.* If you thought the way I thought, you'd feel the way I feel. While the phrase "logical thinking" is used, step 2 really focuses on the feeling produced by that thinking process. When you are at 2, you describe how you feel and why you feel that way. It is at step 2 where you express your emotional reaction.

3. *The data used in the logical thinking process may or may not be valid.* If the things I am thinking are true, then the way I am thinking and feeling is correct. If they are not true then my thoughts and feelings are incorrect. Step 3 is for analysis and problem solving. Emotions are set aside and an objective rational inspection of the operating beliefs is made. These concepts are discussed further in chapter 8, "Helping Your Clients Tell Themselves the Truth."

Burt is hurt and upset because another employee in his firm got a promotion and he didn't. Both his wife Millie and he accept that he is upset and hurt (1). They are on the same frequency—no problem.

Burt says that the boss has it in for him and that the other employee connived with the boss to get the promotion. Burt is at 2. After listening for about a minute, Millie decides that her husband's beliefs are invalid because the promoted employee has more seniority and an advanced degree her husband doesn't have. She interrupts his story and begins to interject her reasoning. She wants him to feel better. If Burt would only look at things the correct way (Millie's way) he wouldn't be so upset.

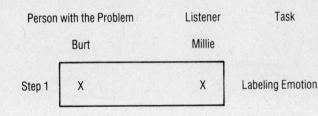

Person with the Problem	Listener	Task
Burt	Millie	
Step 1 X	X	Labeling Emotion

Fig. 6.9   1-2-3 Model

She is at 3. The diagram below summarizes the remainder of the interaction.

This couple started on the same frequency but quickly parted company. Burt went to 2 while Millie went to 3. This type of miscommunication creates hard feelings. The person with the problem doesn't feel heard, understood, or supported. The listener, on the other hand, often believes the other person is being childish and blowing things out of proportion.

Examine your own significant relationships, especially your marriage. How often do you find yourself at 3 when you are the listener? How often do you find yourself at 2 when you have the problem? The universality of this interaction makes this model a useful tool.

In the 1-2-3 model, as with all our communication models, we believe both partners have a responsibility to resolve communication difficulties. While this is true in theory, in practice we find more progress can be made by putting the initial responsibility on the listener. The person with the problem is often so emotionally involved (and upset) that being rational is difficult. The listener, on the other hand, is in much better control.

Our goal is to keep both partners on the same frequency. Both being at step 1 is easy. The person with the problem is already at 2. This is where the responsibility rests on the

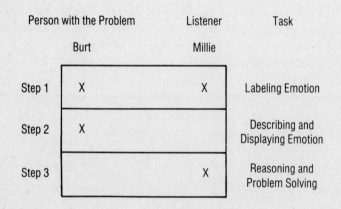

	Person with the Problem	Listener	Task
	Burt	Millie	
Step 1	X	X	Labeling Emotion
Step 2	X		Describing and Displaying Emotion
Step 3		X	Reasoning and Problem Solving

Fig. 6.10   1-2-3 Model - Continued

listener. He or she can choose to remain at step 2 instead of going immediately to 3.

This is best done when the listener does not pass judgment on the reasoning of the other. Instead, he or she wants to find out as much as is possible about what the partner feels and what is causing him or her to feel that way. The listener is interested in what is bothering his or her partner and why. As the person with the problem continues to tell the story, the emotional pressure begins to diminish. Less emotional pressure enables the person to consider other alternative explanations to the problem.

After the problem has been thoroughly heard, the listener has earned the right to move to step 3. He or she has patiently listened, asked clarifying questions, and has been accepting of the answers. Now, it is the listener's turn to examine the beliefs underlying the problem. The listener should proceed cautiously. While the intensity has lessened, the person with the problem probably still feels the same way. When one doesn't feel attacked, he or she will be more open to hearing another perspective.

To summarize the 1-2-3 model, both the person with the problem and the listener acknowledge the feelings being experienced as fact (1). Next, both people explore the beliefs that produce the feelings (2). Finally, both people (usually at the direction of the listener) evaluate the validity of the beliefs (3). Using this sequence, the partners share the same frequencies during the entire discussion. This doesn't mean that there will no longer be differences of opinion. There will be fewer, however. The more time and effort the listener puts into understanding the problem, the more likely he or she will see (and sometimes, even agree with) the other's point of view. The person who feels understood and accepted and who can discharge some of the emotional pressure is more open to considering other interpretations of events.

INTEGRATING NONVERBAL AND VERBAL COMMUNICATION

When a speaker's nonverbal and verbal communication match, there is little confusion about what is meant. When Lon smiles, looks appreciatively, and tells his wife Darla he likes her dress, Darla is likely to believe he means it.

Mixed messages are different. Lon may say, "You look nice, dear," but his head is buried in the paper. The verbal compliment is lost. Did he mean what he said or was the fact that his nose was in the sports page a sign he didn't like the dress?

Megan watched Sol sitting in the pew next to her. The pastor was preaching on the characteristics of the Christian husband. Sol was frowning. Later, he told Megan he liked the sermon. Megan didn't know if she should believe him.

There is a popular misconception that when nonverbal and verbal messages disagree, one should trust the nonverbal. Sometimes trusting the nonverbal is correct, but often it is not. Research has shown that if you determine the true feelings of others based on their nonverbal behavior alone, you will be right only one-third of the time.

We emphasized earlier in this chapter the importance of checking out verbal behavior. It is just as important to check out nonverbal behavior. All you really know when confusing nonverbal behavior occurs is that something is going on. You won't know what is going on unless you ask.

Darla might ask Lon, "Honey, you said you liked my dress but you didn't look at me." "I'm sorry," Lon might reply. "I saw the dress when you were showing it to the kids. I really do like it."

Megan could ask Sol, "You said you liked the pastor's sermon, but you were frowning during the sermon. I'm confused." Sol could respond, "I was thinking how much better my parent's marriage would have been if Dad had followed those principles."

Of course, the answers to Darla's and Megan's questions could have been different. The point is that if the nonverbal and verbal messages do not agree the best way to find out what the real message is, is to ask.

This doesn't mean nonverbal communication is unimportant. It is important. Remember the misconception: When nonverbal and verbal messages disagree, one should trust the nonverbal. Because people tend to believe this, it is important to keep the nonverbal and verbal as congruent as possible. Public speakers know this. They practice making their posture, facial expressions, and tone of voice match their words. You can practice this with your couples. Give them an assigned topic they feel strongly about and coach them to match their nonverbal communication with their verbal communication. When matching improves, overall communication improves.

Summary

There are many models of communication. Most of them have something to offer. We find in our counseling that frequent use of a small number of models is superior to infrequent use of a large number.

We have found the Intent-Impact, Transitional Analysis—Parent, Adult, Child, and the 1-2-3 Model to be among the best. Some of the concepts overlap and none of the concepts contradict.

People who come to counseling often lack communication skills, but their main purpose in coming is to solve other problems. The sooner we can give them some communication skills, the sooner they will be able to use these skills in managing their problems.

To reinforce the communication skills, we will call their attention to their verbal and nonverbal interactions (both positive and negative) and analyze them, using one, two or all of the models. While working on another problem, taking five minutes or so every once in a while to call the person's attention to communication principles, helps these skills become more automatic.

CHAPTER SEVEN

CONFLICT MANAGEMENT

"DON'T LET THE SUN GO DOWN ON YOUR WRATH"

"The age of disposable marriage is over," says a recent article in *Newsweek*. "Instead of divorcing when times get tough couples are working harder at keeping their unions intact. And they are finding that the rewards of matrimony are often worth the effort."[1] The article suggests that a change in attitude seems to be emerging for some couples in the United States.

Divorce is still seen as an option, but Frank F. Furstenberg, a professor of sociology at the University of Pennsylvania, believes that, increasingly, divorce is seen as a last resort. The negative effects of divorce are being considered along with the notion that divorce is the antidote to an unhappy marriage. We can see the victims: ex-wives raising the children alone; men and women trying to start new lives and at the same time deal with the children from the past; children caught between warring parents, to name a few.

Judith Wallerstein, a psychologist and foremost authority on the impact of divorce on children, found after studying sixty divorced couples for ten years that only ten percent of the ex-spouses reported they both had succeeded in improving their lives.

Reported in the *Newsweek* article are characteristics of long-term, successful marriages. Robert and Jeanette Lauer, in a study of 351 couples married 15 years or more, found these characteristics to be important: being friends; having the qualities of integrity, caring, and sensitivity; and having a sense of humor. Underlying these was a sense of commitment to the spouse as an individual and to the couple relationship. The couples occasionally became sidetracked on other issues, such as children, but they ultimately got back to their commitment to the couple relationship.

David Viscott, author of *I Love You, Let's Work it Out,* also puts a great deal of emphasis upon commitment and presents a series of exercises couples can use to determine whether or not they can make that kind of commitment.[2] Along with programs for developing functional communication skills, techniques have been developed to help couples learn to resolve or manage conflicts that arise at various stages of marriage.

Dr. Samuel Pauker and his wife, Miriam Arond, cited in the *Newsweek* article, studied seventy-five couples and found that most of them described the first year of marriage as either the easiest or hardest year of the marriage. Those who said it was the hardest appeared to be the ones who learned how to work things out, while the others did not appear to work through problems. The "working things out" meant learning how to head off difficulties by confronting differences in a constructive way.

CONFLICT MANAGEMENT

By this time in the counseling process, the couple has met the requirements of the first and second levels of the marital pyramid. Any psychopathology is at least understood and controlled and healthy communication patterns are being learned. As the

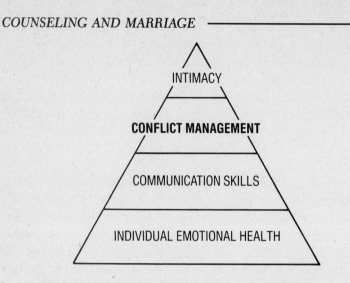

Fig. 7.1   The Third Level of the Pyramid: Conflict Management

counselor, you are not demanding perfect communication but it is desirable that the couple have enough skill to figure out what derails them if their communication train jumps the track. Nowhere will constructive communication be any more important than when dealing with conflict-laden issues.

What Is Conflict Anyway?

When Larry came to counseling, he felt confused. He thought that perhaps he had made a mistake in marrying Helen. They had only been married a few months but it seemed as if they were constantly in conflict, resulting in angry outbursts. He said, "I can't remember ever seeing my parents disagree or argue."

Helen on the other hand had grown up in a family where the members voiced disagreement and differences. They may not have always resolved these differences but at the very least, they voiced them.

Larry had entered marriage with the idea that conflict was bad. His belief was that somehow, magically, they would always agree. However, when two people marry, they bring with them two sets of values, ways of doing things, opinions, preferences, life perspectives, and standards. Sometimes there is agreement and sometimes there is disagreement or differences. At one time or another, problems or conflicts will arise. This need not be bad. Conflicts are an opportunity for growth. Couples can clear the air, bring about creative change, and help get the relationship back on course.

An important starting place for the counselor may be to begin to examine the individual attitudes toward conflict. Is conflict bad? Is conflict a part of married life? Must all conflict be resolved or can it be managed? Can understanding conflict help?

The potential for conflict exists anytime two people interact. Conflict, like many other things, such as anger or fear, is not bad. It is a part of being created uniquely different. What is important is what we choose to do with the conflict.

Does the other person have the right to view things differently? A model using some notions from Eric Berne's Transactional Analysis theory is useful here. Relationships can be viewed from three different perspectives or positions.

Position One: I'm Superior.
I'm okay. I have rights.
You're not okay. You don't have rights.

A person operating from this belief says the other person must do things as he or she believes.

Position Two: I'm Inferior.
You're okay. You have rights.
I'm not okay. I don't have rights.

A person at this position will choose to do what the other person desires without regard for his or her own wishes.

Position Three: We are equal.
I'm okay and you are okay.
We both have rights.

Individuals holding Position 3—*we are equal*—will be open to seeking ways in which they can respect the other's rights and help that person meet his or her needs and desires. At the same time, these individuals will take responsibility for expressing their wants, needs, and desires and for seeing that some of these get worked out in the relationship. These individuals accept the responsibility of working toward meeting both sets of needs. It is from the I'm Okay, You're Okay perspective that the highest degree of overall couple satisfaction will come.

Another very important component of conflict resolution is the development of an attitude that is open to understanding, that is, accepting the other person and how he or she responds to conflict.

Paul Tournier discusses several aspects of getting to understanding.[3] First, the individual must want to understand.

George and Mary had experienced much misunderstanding from the beginning of their relationship because of miscommunication. When they came in, George privately shared with the counselor that he wanted to be out of the relationship and that he no longer loved Mary. Publicly, however, he indicated that he was committed to working on the relationship. The next day George filed for divorce. Individual counseling later revealed George's inability to share real feelings, as opposed to what he thought he should say. (He had come into the marriage with the idea that the way a marriage works is that, no matter what, one must do what the other partner wishes.) In reality, by the time he and Mary had come for counseling he didn't want to work at understanding her. He only wanted to be out of the marriage.

Tournier goes on to state that getting to understanding involves a second characteristic, a willingness to express oneself in a loving, caring manner. This takes courage, because we must deal with differences in order to understand and help the other partner as well as ourselves. Harry's auto-repair business had grown from five days a week to six. Because he was feeling as if he had no time alone, Harry started staying home Sunday mornings to watch football, which in his part of the country, came on television on Sunday mornings. Mary understood, but she had some concerns. And she wanted to share these in a loving and caring way. She said, "I know that you have a good relationship with God. I know you are not being rebellious. But it would really please me if you would come to church with us half of the time. I understand your need for time alone, but I'm afraid the children don't understand your not going to church."

The work presented by Jordan and Margaret Paul is very useful in helping couples develop an understanding of what sometimes goes on during conflict. The Pauls believe we have been programmed to respond to conflict in one of two general ways.[4] The way most of us have been programmed from early childhood on, is to be protective of ourselves as opposed to learning ways in which we can begin to discover the whys, hows, and whats connected to conflict.

We protect ourselves by withdrawing, blaming, defending, and controlling. On the other hand, we can discover ourselves and others by developing questions that allow us to consider why a person is upset or what might be the issues. A schematic we use for this is shown below.

If the individuals in the marriage relationship can begin to understand protecting and discovering types of programming, they can begin to develop an attitude of openness and discovery that can give them concrete information to use in resolving or managing conflict.

We have simplified the Pauls's work a great deal. They go on to describe three different positions people use to protect themselves—control, compliance, and indifference. When both

Conflict
Methods of Responding

To Protect Oneself	To Discover Self & Others
Action: Blaming Defending Controlling Withdrawing	**Action:** Asking *Why am I upset?* *What are my issues?* *Why is she upset?* *What may be her issues?*

| To avoid pain and rejection | To gain understanding |

Fig. 7.2 Protect - Discover Model

partners are protecting themselves, which is what usually happens, there are four possible patterns.

One is *control-compliance*. In this case, one tries to reduce conflict by being in control, and the other person reduces conflict by giving in.

A second pattern is *control-control*. Each partner believes that if he or she were in control, things would be better.

The third pattern is *control-indifference*. One partner tries to control and the other says, "Okay, let him do it; it doesn't really make any difference."

The fourth pattern is *indifference-indifference*. In this case both withdraw from the situation in order to lessen the hurt.

If all four of the conflict patterns are a result of each person protecting himself or herself, the counselor must help each person replace the protective stance with an open one. An open relationship is one where both people are willing to discover and share their own fears, motives, and desires as well as those of the partner. The willingness to expose oneself to the other is reinforced by receiving acceptance and understanding.

The first step, when working with the control-compliance pattern, is to help the compliant person express his or her true feelings. Often the control person is not aware that the compliant person has different feelings. The next step is to help the control person to share decision-making responsibilities. The negotiation and compromise tools presented in this chapter will be useful for this couple.

Conflict is much more apparent in the control-control pattern. The woman and man are clearly aware that they disagree. A useful concept to use with the control-control couple is, "You can win the battle but lose the war." Several years ago this conversation with an acquaintance occurred. "Hi Mandy, how is it going?" "Terrible," Mandy said. "My husband just filed for a divorce. I won one too many arguments!" The control person needs to know that marriage is not a win-lose proposition. In marriage there are either two winners or two losers. People with a high need for control often have black-and-white, good-or-bad, right-or-wrong thinking. Their way is white, good, and right. They need to see that because their partners view things differently, they are not black, bad, and wrong. We point out that most conflict is not between a right position and a wrong position, but between two differing points of view, neither of which is totally right or totally wrong. Differences are frequently just a matter of preference. We remind these couples that Baskin-Robbins has thirty-one flavors. If there were only one right flavor, the other thirty would be unnecessary.

The control-indifference pattern usually begins as control-compliance. The compliant person gets tired of giving in. Further protection is achieved by distancing himself or herself from the controlling partner. Control doesn't hurt as much when one doesn't care. In this situation the control person must realize that the partner has moved away because of his or her controlling. Learning to relinquish control is the key element. Compromise and trade-off techniques are also useful in helping this couple.

The indifference-indifference couple is the most discouraged of all. Each has hurt and been hurt by the other. They have backed off to lessen the possibility of further hurt. Helping the indifferent-indifferent couple to uncritically accept each other's differences, to communicate personal feelings and desires, and to negotiate mutual agreement can move them to an open relationship.

Later in this chapter we discuss aggressive, assertive, and passive behaviors. The compliant person is usually passive. The control person is usually either aggressive or assertive-negative. The indifferent person, regardless of earlier style, has become passive. The suggested remedies for changing the undesirable style (aggressive, assertive-negative and passive-negative) are useful in changing the control, compliant, and indifferent marital patterns.

The last attitudinal question asks whether all conflict needs to be resolved, or can a couple learn to manage the conflict. We believe there are times when a mutually-agreed-upon resolution works. For example, the question of which movie to see comes up. Teddy doesn't care for romantic themes and Marjorie dislikes war stories, but they both enjoy adventure movies. Adventure movies can be the preferred choice. In this case, resolution has taken place by mutual agreement.

At times the best solution is management. For example, the

two of us respond to minor crisis situations differently. Dee's first response is to catastrophize about the situation. Let us suppose we are cooking dinner together and the potatoes burn.

> Dee: "Oh no, how could that happen. I can't believe it. I just can't believe that could happen. What a waste. Supper is going to be ruined."

> Ruby: "It happened. Let's clean it up. We can fix some toast instead."

We will probably never respond to crises in the same manner. Potential for conflict exists here. If Ruby gives Dee a few minutes to get his world in perspective, he calms down and everything is fine. If, on the other hand, Ruby responds with criticism of his catastrophizing rather than acceptance, it takes him longer to get over the incident. Then we have hard feelings between us. A part of managing this conflict is for one person to give the other person time to work through reactions, anger, and fears. (How to manage anger will be discussed later.) That is, we must make a decision to allow the other person to handle frustrations in his or her way, and not interfere. For us, giving that time and space usually results in control of the person's own issues. After that has happened, we then can begin to talk about problem solving around the crisis rather than around the individual's reactions.

To briefly summarize, the counselor may find it useful to explore with the couple their attitudes toward conflict, toward the rights of others, toward understanding conflict, and toward potential outcomes of conflict.

WILL ASSERTIVENESS HELP OR HAMPER?

We include a discussion of assertiveness in this chapter because nonassertive behavior often intensifies existing conflict or is actually responsible for the conflict.

Assertiveness is related to the individual personality and therefore affects the first three levels of the pyramid—individual emotional health, communication skills, and conflict management. And a person's level of assertiveness influences what is communicated and how he or she goes about resolving conflict.

Assertiveness is best understood in comparison with nonassertive behavior and attitudes. People easily accept passive behavior as being nonassertive but have difficulty seeing aggressive behavior as nonassertive. Assertive behavior (assertive-positive to be exact) is the psychologically healthy and biblically sound point of balance between the two extremes. Figure 7.3 graphically shows this balance.

Aggressive.   I count, you don't. My needs are important, yours are not. I want my needs met and if yours are not, tough! I'm selfish, I don't care.

Assertive-Negative.   I count and you count. I'm important and so are you. We both have needs and wants. We have equal rights. Let's work it out cooperatively; our own needs will be met by helping each other. The problem is, I get so focused on my needs that I don't think about what yours are. I'm not selfish, because I do care, but I may look selfish sometimes because I am so self-focused.

Assertive-Positive.   I count and you count. I'm important and so are you. We both have needs and wants. We have equal rights. Let's work cooperatively in getting our needs met by helping each other. I'll try to place myself in your shoes. I frequently ask myself whether what I'm asking for is fair. I try to do the things I think you would like. I won't be a martyr though. I'm not a mind reader. I won't know many of your needs unless you tell me.

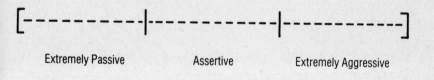

Extremely Passive   Assertive   Extremely Aggressive

Fig. 7.3   Assertive Continuum

Passive-Positive. I count and you count. I'm important, so are you. We both have needs and wants. We have equal rights. I believe all this but I have a hard time asking for what I want and a hard time saying no to what I don't want. I want you to give me what I want and not ask me to do what I don't want to. If you don't meet my needs I'll keep quiet, but it will bother me. If you ask more of me than I want to give, I'll do it, but I'll get resentful. I'll stuff all my negative feelings for a while; then I'll explode. I'll go from passive to aggressive. Then I'll feel guilty and move back to passive.

Passive-Negative. I don't count. I'm not worth much. If bad things happen to me, I probably deserve them. I'm not going to ask for what I want because I don't have it coming. If you give me what I want without my asking, I'll just feel guilty.

Most of us spend some time in each of these five categories, but fortunately we do not spend much time either as an aggressive or passive-negative. From the clients we've sampled, the most common position is passive-positive. The second most common is assertive-negative. The one we are aiming for is assertive-positive.

We can help the passive-positives become assertive by giving them permission to assert themselves. They are reminded (you can instruct them to say) that it is important to have a positive mental attitude about oneself. "I need to count with me. It is healthy for me to see my wants and desires as legitimate. Furthermore, it is important that I make my desires known to my partner."

The individual working on becoming more assertive must first understand what is assertive behavior. For example, it is legitimate to expect the workload to be shared. It's okay to get your way some of the time without having to justify. It is acceptable to say no, when saying yes means giving up *you*. Knowing what assertive behavior is will not automatically produce feelings that say it is okay to be assertive. Earlier programming has conditioned us to feel uncomfortable being assertive. The way to change these uncomfortable feelings is to practice assertive behaviors even though it feels uncomfortable or wrong. Most skiers probably felt uncomfortable and unnatural the first time they were on skis. In order to practice, the person begins with a decision to do so. During the practicing, self-talk is used to remind oneself that he or she is doing the right thing, even though it feels uncomfortable. Some people require a long period of practicing before they become comfortable.

It is interesting that as Christians we are admonished to bring all our needs before the Lord. Even though God knows all our needs, wants, and hurts, we are still told to ask. If an all-knowing God wants us to ask, it certainly makes sense that our fallible, nonmindreading spouses need us to ask even more.

We have found that with practice the passive person becomes more comfortable being assertive. We find if both partners are less than assertive-positive, working on increasing assertiveness is a good couple-counseling task. Monitoring each other's success at being assertive is a good homework assignment.

On the other hand, if one partner is very nonassertive (aggressive, passive-positive in the extreme or passive-negative) individual work is desirable.

The assertive-negative person can be helped most by his or her passive partner becoming more assertive. The assertive-negative person has positive (assertive) beliefs and attitudes but some negative (egocentric or self-focused) behavior. If the formerly passive spouse becomes more assertive (is now asking for what he or she wants) the assertive-negative person will have the needed information with which to behave more equitably. The long-suffering passive-positive spouse reinforces the negative side of the assertive-negative partner. The long-suffering passive-positive parent reinforces or even helps create the assertive-negative or aggressive child by giving everything the person wants. This is especially true if the parents deny their own needs in the process.

If we see a couple with whom lack of assertiveness is an issue, we will request that they (yes, both, even though only one of them has assertiveness problems) do some outside reading. Two books we recommend are: *Your Perfect Right* by Robert Alberti and Michael Emmonds and *Beyond Assertiveness* by John Faul and David Augsburger.[5]

TOOLS FOR CONFLICT MANAGEMENT

As was stated earlier, conflict occurs when two people want two different things. It frequently is not an issue of right or wrong and good or bad. It is an issue of preference—a matter of taste. Conflict is resolved or managed when both partners agree that the choice made is satisfactory—not necessarily ideal, but satisfactory to both of them.

Compromise

Compromise is not a dirty word, as in, "he compromised his values." Of course, a moral compromise is negative. A relational compromise, on the other hand, is usually positive. It is giving up some individual gain for the gain of the relationship. There are several types of compromise: mathematical, relational, and trade-off.

Mathematical Compromise. Whenever numbers are involved, mathematical compromise is possible. For example, Maggie would like to spend $50 of their $200 surplus income (after fixed expenses are paid) each month for entertainment and put $150 into savings. Rich would reverse the order. He believes that they are young and that their income will only increase over the years. He wants to spend $150 for entertainment and $50 for savings. A good compromise, and one that would probably please both Maggie and Rich, is to put $100 into savings and $100 into entertainment.

In another example, Hans and Gerte are discussing the frequency of love-making. Gerte would like to make love four times a week. Hans is satisfied with twice a week. One wants four, one wants two; three is the average. It is a little more than one wants and a little less than the other wants. However, it is acceptable to both.

The mathematical compromise can work as long as the numbers are not too far apart. In the savings-entertainment example, it could have worked for a $175–$25 split almost as well as a $150–$50 split. However, a $200 entertainment to $0 savings is different. Individual therapy is probably necessary when one person is all play and no work, while the other person is all work and no play. If the issues involve how much or how often, the mathematical compromise usually works.

Relational Compromise. In this type of compromise the relationship itself contributes to the overall happiness or satisfaction. For example, José's favorite food is Italian. Ronni prefers Chinese. If José eats alone, he chooses Italian. If she eats alone in a restaurant, she chooses Chinese. If they eat together, they usually choose Mexican. Why? They both like Mexican food (although not as well as their first choices). More importantly, they know the other person also likes Mexican food.

We use this diagram to show that in a relationship, there are three parts: myself, the other (him or her), and the couple (both of us). When I am alone, I may consider only myself. When I am with the other person, my happiness comes from myself plus both of us.

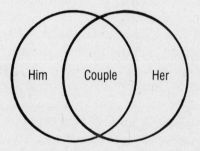

Fig. 7.4   Him, Her, and Couple Compromise

Looking at José and Ronni in this context, we will rate each type of food on a scale of 1 to 100.

	Him	Her	Couple	Total Him	Total Her
Italian	95	20	35	130	55
Chinese	20	95	35	55	130
Mexican	85	75	80	165	155

In the relational compromise our happiness comes from combining our individual happiness with the couple happiness. If Rachel is an ardent baseball fan (she rates baseball a 99), how much fun is it to go to a ball game with Robert who hates (he rates baseball a 1) the game? Is the average of 99 and 1 a 50? Not in this case. When we are with someone who really dislikes what we like, the overall enjoyment is lowered. The "couple" part of a 99–1 split is more like 10 than 50. In a relationship we are not seeking only to get our way. Yes, we would like that when possible; but we want the other person to be happy also.

How do Rachel and Robert resolve their differences? The key is to find an activity they both enjoy even though it may not be either person's first choice. If Robert and Rachel rate tennis an 85 and 75, respectively, watching tennis would be a good activity for this couple. With a "him" score of 85 and a "her" score of 75, the "couple" score for tennis is 80. This would give Rachel a total score of 155 (75 + 80) and Robert a total score of 165 (85 + 80). Also, Rachel doesn't have to give up her love for baseball. She can watch an occasional game when she and Robert are not doing a "couple" activity.

In the cases of José and Ronni and Rachel and Robert, each gained happiness from combining their personal happiness with the "couple" happiness. This concept is vital! In a healthy relationship our total happiness is a combination of personal happiness plus the together or "couple" happiness, which is determined by the personal happiness of the other person as well.

The relational compromise is one in which an individual's second or even third choice can be better than the first choice. The secret ingredient comes from how happy my second or third choice is going to make my partner.

Trade-Offs. A trade-off is another form of compromise. Not all things can be mathematically divided. The trade-off involves either taking turns or making an exchange.

Taking turns is, "I'll take the kids to the game, if you'll pick them up." "If you give the kids their baths this week, I'll do it next week." "You can choose the TV programs every odd month and I'll choose every even month." An exchange is, "I'll visit your parents without complaining if you will teach our son to drive." "I'll have the office dinner here if you will paint the living and dining rooms." "I'll go without complaining to an occasional gun show if you will go without complaining to an occasional antique show."

Any form of compromise, whether it be mathematical,

relational, or trade-off, can allow two people with different interests, values, and desires to live more harmoniously with each other.

The Modality Check

Robert Weiss developed what he refers to as a modality check (see the flow chart that follows) for conflict resolution.[6] The intent is to help the partners do two things: determine the need of the spouse and determine how the couple could handle the particular need. (What does the partner want from me?)

There usually are two general modes—expressing emotions or problem-solving. Does he want to express emotions or solve the problem? That is, does he want to be understood or does he want to fight? If he wants to fight, a time-out is appropriate. You do need to arrange for a time-in when each partner has calmed down and has reached the point of wanting to be understood. At this point then, appropriate speaking and listening skills are used.

The second want mode is that of resolving a conflict. There are two kinds of conflict: external and internal. An internal conflict is between the partners. This requires discussing a desired behavior change in one or both spouses. Is this change acceptable? If so, implement it. If not, negotiate. An external problem is one outside the couple relationship. In this case, the partner needs to be listened to and needs to hear reflections of his or her feelings. If the partner desires suggestions or help (you need to ask for permission to do so), then suggestions or help may be given. Using the 1-2-3 communication model would be helpful here.

The information in this flow chart may seem obvious. However, time and time again, couples move into conflict because they fail to determine the need of the other spouse.

Susan dreaded 5:30 when it was time for Dereck to return home from his research and development job. She knew he would be tense because of his frustration at having to work for someone who seemed to hold an opposite opinion on about everything. Every time Susan offered suggestions, Dereck would get angry. She really didn't know what to do.

Susan: Dereck, you look frustrated and tired. Is there something I can do to help?

Dereck: The most helpful thing would be to let me ventilate. If I could just express my frustrations of the day, then I believe I could forget about things at work for the rest of the evening. I don't believe problem solving will help, but listening will.

Structured Communication

Most counselors will be confronted with what we call the over- and under-talkers. There may be several different scenarios. One might say, "My husband uses logic and basically over- or outtalks me. I can't think as quickly or logically as he does, therefore, I can't defend my position. And we end up doing what he wants. Or, the husband might say, "I just keep talking until she does what I want." Or, "My wife just keeps talking and it is like it is never going to end. So, I just give in."

A technique that can be useful for such couples is structured communication. In this technique, the couple identifies the problem area or topic to be discussed. One partner is assigned the role of the speaker and the other becomes the listener. The speaker gets five minutes to present thoughts—not accusations, blames, or judgments, but why it is important, what are the concerns, and how they might accomplish whatever it is.

The listener's task is to listen. That means he is not talking, nor is he planning what he is going to say in rebuttal. He may take a few notes to later jog his memory; however, he maintains good eye contact.

When five minutes are up, the listener gets a couple of minutes to ask clarifying questions only. Clarifying questions are ones that ask for more information such as, "You stated thus and so. Is this what you mean?" "Help me understand what you meant by . . . . ?" It is the speaker's responsibility to clarify.

When clarification is completed, they exchange roles. The speaker becomes the listener and the listener becomes the speaker. They then repeat the process.

If they are ready to move to problem solving they do so. Or

Flow Chart for Conflict Resolution

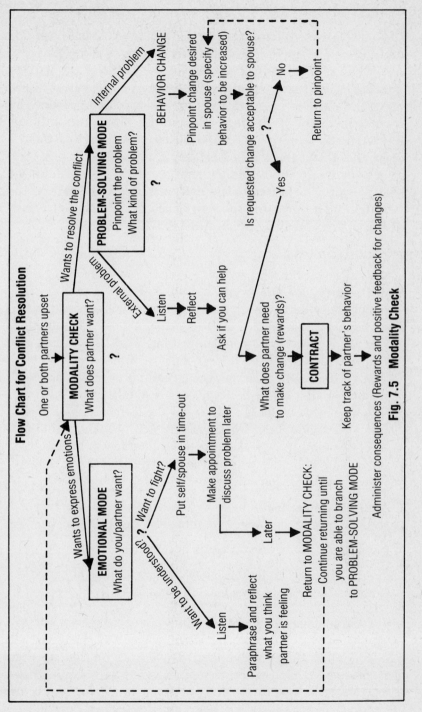

Fig. 7.5   Modality Check

they may need to request time to think about what has been said and agree upon another time to have another session.

The greatest benefit of this technique is that each partner gets the opportunity to express ideas and to feel heard. The counselor's office is a good place for the couple to practice this technique in the beginning, because the procedure will feel awkward for some people. The office practice gives them a sense that they can do it. When they choose to do this on their own time it will be useful for them to choose a time and place that will provide privacy. The end of the day may not be the best time. The greatest success comes from a loving, caring attitude. The following illustrates a practice session.

Counselor: The subject of the family budget has come up several times. But we have not seemed to make any progress in this area. What I would like to do today is provide an opportunity for you each to express your thoughts and concerns about this topic. I am suggesting we use a technique known as structured communication. That simply means that one of you will be the speaker, the other the listener. The speaker will talk on the agreed-upon topic for five minutes giving his or her concerns and ideas. This will be followed by a couple of minutes for the listener to ask clarifying questions about what was said, with the intent being to understand the speaker. Joan, I'd like you to be the listener, and Bob, you will be the first speaker. Let's determine what the focus will be.

Joan: I would like to focus on the possibility of the two of us cooperating on budget planning and executing.

Counselor: Bob, do you agree to this focus?

Bob: I'll agree to talking about the possibility of cooperating on the budget even though I'm not for it.

Bob presents his views. His major point is concern about possible nagging and blaming. He is also concerned that Joan will not want to do things as he does. "If we work on this together, I'm concerned that it will turn into a nagging and blaming time. I'll be told that how I'm trying to stretch an income that is less than our outgo is wrong. Therefore, to avoid hassle I prefer to decide by myself. It's the man's job anyway. I want to have the final word.

Joan: (clarifying) Are you saying that the main reason you don't wish me to be a part of the budgeting process is that you fear the nagging and criticizing I will do?

Bob: Yes.

Joan: Bob, please help me understand the importance to you that it is the husband's role to handle the finances.

Bob: I really don't feel that handling the finances must be the man's job. But I do get scared of losing too much control. Maybe you won't need me anymore.

Joan: Bob, are you concerned that I want to take over?

Bob: Maybe, and that maybe you won't need me.

Bob and Joan now exchange the speaker and listener roles.

Joan: Bob, you are important to me. I desire (choose) to be with you and to grow old with you. It is not my intent to take over our finances. I don't know that I could do better than you are doing. But it is important to me to be a part of the process. Things that I imagine, because I don't know, almost always seem worse than they are. So, I get scared and I protect myself by nagging. (This is an example of the Pauls's process of taking the risk of getting in touch with and sharing underlying fears and feelings. "I'm scared you might not need me." This is the process of discovery. Joan continues her speaker role.)

Joan: There are several reasons I'd like to be a part of the budgeting process. If I know what hasn't been paid, I can at least be prepared for the "lack of payment" phone calls. But more than that, perhaps I will see ways that I can help cut down the outgo. I'm willing to do that if you are.

She goes on to talk about the need to know about the family finances if something were to happen to Bob, plus the need to know about how they are planning for retirement. It is important to her to know that if she writes a check it won't bounce. She goes on, "I get really tired of not being able to trust anything."

Bob: (clarifying) One of the things I think I'm hearing is that it would give you a sense of security to know what's happening financially, even if it isn't good news. Is that right?

Joan: Yes.

Bob: Joan, I do not believe I am ready to talk about a solution because at this point I don't know if I can trust the situation to not turn into a "blame Bob" session. Can you give me some time to think about this. Maybe we can talk about it next week here, but I don't want to talk about it before then.

Counselor: I'd like to compliment you both for staying on the subject. Also, for asking for what you want and need and stating what you fear. One thing I'd like you to think about between now and next week is a specific plan as to how you might work at budgeting together. As you think about this, focus upon what specific behaviors might be useful.

The counselor may need to spend several sessions helping the couple refine this technique so eventually they can use a less formal method. We believe it is a useful technique. However, couples need a lot of help in shaping, understanding, and practicing it.

Ten Commandments for Fighting Fair

Marriages fail for various reasons—lack of communication, differences in parenting style, lack of agreement on how to spend money, and so forth. One thing that seems to be a common factor in each of these areas is a sense of inequity. It has been speculated that the real reason behind many divorces is that one partner does not feel he or she is getting a fair share in some important matter. Both partners may feel this way.

Obviously, before a sense of unfairness can be dealt with, it must be communicated. Assuming the unfairness issue has been communicated, the offending partner has a responsibility to resolve this issue with his or her partner. An attempt at resolution is necessary even if the offending partner doesn't agree with the other partner's perception.

"Therefore, if you are offering your gift at the altar and there remember that your brother has something against you, leave your gift there in front of the altar. First go and be reconciled to your brother; then come and offer your gift."   (Matt. 5:23–24)

Dealing with unfairness or inequity in the marriage is difficult for couples. It is as difficult for the person who is accused of being unfair as it is for the one who believes he or she is being treated unfairly. We believe that giving young couples some guidelines to follow is useful in working through these issues. Lisa Engelhardt has written "The Ten Commandments for Fighting Fair," which can be helpful in dealing with real or imagined inequities in the marriage relationship.[7] The following is a part of her work on the subject:

1. *Make an appointment.* The time and place should be agreeable to both parties. ". . . . let not the sun go down upon your wrath" (Eph. 4:26 KJV).

2. *State the real issue.* The real issue in an argument can be elusive, even for the most practiced fair fighters. State (a) the offending action + (b) my feelings about it + (c) its impact on me.

3. *Use "I" statements.* "I" statements state our case neutrally, nonjudgmentally, rationally. "I feel frustrated when the sink is always full of dirty dishes."

4. *Express honest feelings.* We are not always good at this because we've been taught there are good feelings and bad feelings. In reality, feelings just are. Feelings are fact. It is fair to report fact.

5. *Listen.* Listening in fighting fair means we are on the edges of our chairs waiting to discover the other's thoughts

and feelings. Therefore, we are not concerned with being right.

6. *Laugh at yourself.* It is hard to laugh in the midst of conflict. However, humor reminds us of good will between us. It reduces tension and threat. Be careful, however; there is a fine line between humor and sarcasm.

7. *Stay calm.* If the conflict escalates, it may be necessary to repeat the original issues. If it seems a fight is inevitable, a truce may need to be called. Postpone the discussion until a later mutually agreed-upon time.

8. *Come up with creative solutions.* Brainstorm ideas, examine consequences, and select a plan to be used and evaluated.

9. *Make a covenant.* Just as God set a rainbow in the sky as a sign of covenant—the conflicts end, the reconciliation, the promise—we, too, offer gestures to seal our covenants after conflicts. Apologize if necessary. The make-up kiss, hugs, flowers, or cards are gestures.

10. *Lovingly forget and be friends.* "[Love] . . . keeps no record. . ." (1 Cor. 13:5). Our reservoir of forgiveness must be endless. As we struggle to let go of hurt we must remember that forgiveness is a process. If we have fun together and communicate regularly, then we create a climate of love, respect, and trust that will foster productive confrontations in the future.

The concepts presented in "The Ten Commandments for Fighting Fair" are useful for all types of marital conflict, not just those that center around unfairness or inequity.

When One Partner Won't Participate

There are times when one partner refuses to be a part of resolving the conflict. Yet, he or she chooses to remain in the relationship. What can be done? We tell our clients the following:

Perhaps the very first thing is to *accept the fact that one person can't change the other person.* We often put a lot of energy into trying to do this very thing. Know what your own issues are before trying to change things. This will require clarifying your own thoughts and feelings. What kind of partner are you? Are you nagging or are you loving? Are your expectations realistic? Are you behaving in a Christlike manner? Know what you will and won't do in the relationship. *Assume responsibility for your part of the relationship.* Stand behind your position firmly and clearly without becoming rigid, defensive, or insulting, or without blaming or attacking the other person.

These notions are discussed in *The Dance of Anger: A Woman's Guide to Changing Patterns of Intimate Relationships.*[8] Another useful book in this subject area is *How to Save Your Marriage Alone.*[9]

ANGER MANAGEMENT

Anger can be a couple issue, an individual issue, or both. We are going to address anger as a couple issue here and as an individual issue in the next chapter.

Anger as a couple issue refers to the reaction of the second person to the first person's anger. We are not concerned here (although we will be in the next chapter) with whether the first person's anger is justified. Anger as a couple issue is concerned with how the original anger gets inflamed by the reaction of the spouse.

Degrees of Anger

Not everyone is aware that emotions come in degrees. A distinction is made between annoyance or irritation, and anger. One is still rational and able to reason when annoyed or irritated. When one is angry, the ability to reason, to see other alternatives or to see another point of view is impaired. When one is angry (as contrasted with being annoyed or irritated) the voice is louder and the posture and facial cues are hard or rigid. Irrational thinking is evidenced by a closed-mindedness and critical or blaming attitude, by jumping to conclusions, exaggerating the unimportant, or minimizing the important. If someone is a little angry, the above is seen to a lesser degree; but if someone is very angry, the above is seen to a greater degree.

The most significant point is that an angry person is irrational. By definition, then, an angry person is not to be reasoned with and yet, what do we usually do when our spouse is angry with us? We try to reason.

Tom: You really tick me off! I leave the house at seven in the morning, work hard all day, get home at six and find the place looks worse than when I left. What do you do all day? I'm going to take out the cotton-picking phone! Do you ever watch the kids? Their stuff is all over the front yard and driveway.

If you were Karen, Tom's wife, what would you be feeling? What would you like to say to Tom? Four common responses to Tom would be to: (a) justify why the house and yard wasn't immaculate, (b) apologize for the same, (c) counterattack, mentioning some of Tom's weaknesses, or (d) angrily withdraw, using the silent treatment.

If Karen justifies at this point, she is casting her pearls before swine. Even if her justification is valid Tom will not be able to hear it. In fact, Tom will see her reasoning as an excuse to get out of trouble and it will make him madder. When the other person is angry, an attempt to justify is likely to increase the anger.

If Karen apologizes, Tom will question her motive. Tom has a head of steam in his pressure cooker. He wants to let it out by blasting Karen. If she apologizes, what will Tom do with his anger? He believes her apology to be an insincere attempt to get out of trouble. When the other person is angry, a quick apology is likely to increase the anger.

If Karen counterattacks, it will be as though she poured gasoline on the fire. An attack on his family, earning power, or masculinity would inflame Tom. When the other person is angry, a counterattack is likely to increase the anger.

If Karen angrily withdraws either by stomping out of the house or by just giving Tom the silent treatment, things will get worse. When the other person is angry, an angry withdrawal is likely to increase the anger.

Active Listening

If justifying, apologizing, counterattacking, or angrily withdrawing only increase anger, what is left? There is no way to make another's anger instantly go away. There is a process, though, that can slowly reduce the other's anger. This process is called *active listening.*

To our knowledge, active listening was first described by Thomas Gordon in *Parent Effectiveness Training.* [10] Active listening is a neutral position. When you are listening active you are neither agreeing nor disagreeing. You are merely collecting data. You are trying to find out what the other person believes and feels. While active listening can be used with a variety of emotional states (euphoria to depression), it is especially useful in dealing with anger.

Let's see how Karen might have used active listening with Tom. Please reread Tom's vindictive accusations. Then return to Karen's active listening response.

Karen: You seem to feel that I'm not doing my share. That you have to work ten hours a day while I'm on the phone with my friends and family.

Tom: Well, what else am I to think? The place is a mess.

Karen: (resisting the urge to justify) Do you feel that I don't do my share?

Tom: Yeah, I guess that is the way I feel.

Karen: Do you feel that way all the time?

Tom: (looking and sounding a little less angry) Well, no. Most of the time I don't feel that way. I suppose I resent working all day and then seeing that you didn't do any work.

Karen: Let's see if I understand. Most of the time you feel okay because you see me doing my share; but when it appears that I'm not, that upsets you.

Tom: Yeah. And maybe I shouldn't be. I mean usually you are good about picking things up (most of the anger is gone).

Karen: Tom, was there any other reason you were mad at me besides the mess?

Tom: Well, I was a little hurt by the fact we had talked about making love early last evening; then you got involved with the kids' school projects and didn't get to bed until late. It seems that the kids get the long end of the stick while I get the short end.

Karen: So you feel I've let you down in a couple of ways. (Tom nods.) Honey, I apologize for last night. I was in the mood after supper but I just lost track of time. I'm willing to work on that not happening again but I'll need your help. Tom, about the yard. I should have called your office to warn you. I know how important a clean front yard and driveway are to you, especially when you are tired. I wasn't playing today. I was very productive until about 4:30 when Robin came by with her kids. I helped her hem a couple of her dresses. While we were both tied up our two and her three got every toy out.

Tom: Honey, I'm sorry I jumped all over you. You're right. If I had known what I was walking into, I would have been prepared.

Tom has a problem with jumping to conclusions and exploding. Karen knew this. But instead of attacking him for it, she listened, asked questions, summarized, and clarified until his anger subsided.

When Tom was calmer she could then apologize for what she felt responsible for, but nothing else. And Tom is now able to accept the apology. Karen followed the apology with an explanation of those things Tom was ignorant or misinformed about. He was now able to accept her explanation as valid.

If we can face the other person's anger by active listening, the anger dissipates more rapidly than by other approaches. Even though the other's unfair anger may trigger initial anger in us, we find that as we force ourselves into the active listening mode, our initial anger subsides, and we truly try to understand the other's point of view.

Accepting One Another

One of the most useful tools in conflict resolution, especially anger management, is learning to accept each other. Intimacy is impossible without it. Acceptance has two aspects: acceptance of the person and acceptance of the behavior.

Acceptance of the person, in spite of the behavior, is clearly modeled by Jesus. The adulterous woman (John 8:11) was told that she was not condemned even though her behavior was sinful. I can communicate to my spouse that he or she is a person of worth even though I believe a specific behavior to be wrong.

Clearly, there are behaviors that are wrong by God's or human definition. However, most spouse behaviors that irritate and frustrate our counselees are not illegal, immoral or unethical. People have different priorities, standards of excellence, and ways of doing things. It is not wrong to vacuum every day. Neither is it wrong to make the bed only when the sheets are changed.

We believe it is nearly an absolute necessity to accept the other person. We also believe that the more we can accept each other's behavior, the happier the marriage will be. A quote from *Please Understand Me* sums up how we feel about acceptance:

Different Drums and Different Drummers

If I do not want what you want, please try not to tell me that my want is wrong.

Or if I believe other than you, at least pause before you correct my view.

Or if my emotion is less than yours, or more, given the same circumstances, try not to ask me to feel more strongly or weakly.

Or yet if I act, or fail to act in the manner of your design for action, let me be.

I do not, for the moment at least, ask you to understand me. That will come only when you are willing to give up changing me into a copy of you.

I may be your spouse, your parent, your offspring, your friend, or your colleague. If you will allow me any of my own wants, or emotions, or beliefs, or actions, then you open yourself, so that some day these ways of mine might not seem so wrong, and might finally appear to you as right—for me. To put up with me is the first step to understanding me. Not that you embrace my ways as right for you, but that you are no longer irritated or disappointed with me for my seeming waywardness. And in understanding me you might come to prize my differences from you, and, far from seeking to change me, preserve and even nurture those differences.[11]

Summary

Conflict, two people wanting two different things, is a normal occurrence. In some cases conflict can be resolved by mutual agreement or a compromise in which each person wins. There are other situations in which conflict is managed, not resolved. In these situations, we can agree to disagree. Conflict is most satisfactorily dealt with when egalitarian attitudes and assertive behaviors are present. Much conflict arises from defending our turfs and egos. Admitting our imperfections, then, can keep many fights from ever occurring.

Learning how to compromise, checking out the other person's intentions, using structured communication and rules for fair fighting are useful ways to reduce conflict. The greatest conflict reducer of all is to accept both the other person and his or her ways of doing things.

CHAPTER EIGHT

HELPING YOUR CLIENTS TELL THEMSELVES THE TRUTH

Believing what is not true leads to misunderstandings, which lead to miscommunication, which leads to conflict. Many negative emotions, such as anxiety, depression, jealousy, insecurity, and anger, result from telling ourselves things that are not true.

Sometimes we work with a couple who look healthy psychologically and have had adequate exposure to conflict-management and communication skills. Yet, they can't seem to make progress on their marriage. We suspect problems due to faulty perceptions. Perhaps they are not telling themselves the truth. This often becomes evident as the counselor encourages the couple to replay their last three-day fight, statement by statement. The persons believe their statements, but they often have little or no evidence to back up what is said. People seldom believe things that simply can't be true; however, they frequently believe things that could be true even though they are not.

Our task is to help persons believe only those things that are true or, at least, which have a very high probability of being true. Let's explore some biblical concepts of being truthful with ourselves.

AS A MAN THINKS IN HIS HEART, SO IS HE

Proverbs 23:7 (KJV) said it first and it has not been improved on. What I (a man or a woman) think in my heart—in other words—what I believe, determines how I feel and how I behave. The Greek philosopher Epictetus (who was also a convert to Christianity and a contemporary of the apostle Paul) said that it is the view we take of events rather than the events themselves, that causes us difficulties.

If you walk into a room full of people, many of whom look up at you, what do you conclude? *They are wondering who this attractive person is?* Or, *they see a homely, unwanted intruder?* Your conclusion, not the actual thoughts of the people, leads you to hold your head high or makes you want to crawl into a hole.

In Philippians 4:8, Paul uses several phrases, but only two categories:

> Finally, brethren, whatsoever things are true, whatsoever things are honest, whatsoever things are just, whatsoever things are pure, whatsoever things are lovely, whatsoever things are of good report; if there be any virtue and if there be any praise, think on these things. (KJV)

The two categories Paul uses are: whatever is true (true and honest) and whatever is positive (just, pure, lovely, good report, virtue, and praise). It is no mistake, in our way of thinking, that Paul gave the first admonition to truthfulness and the second to being positive.

Paul may not have been positive always, because life's circumstances were not always positive. However, Paul did not magnify the negative. He did not engage in self-pity. He gave us his truthful reporting of events, first in his own interpretation to himself and then to us, through the Scriptures. The following is a beautiful example of describing life as it is, truthfully, but with optimism.

We are troubled on every side, yet not distressed; we are perplexed, but not in despair; persecuted, but not forsaken; cast down, but not destroyed. (2 Cor. 4:8–9 KJV)

Why was Paul troubled, perplexed, persecuted and cast down but not distressed, in despair, forsaken and destroyed? Weren't things bad enough? We believe things were bad, but Paul neither exaggerated his problems nor magnified the negative. Whenever possible Paul emphasized the positive.

For our light affliction, which is but for a moment, worketh for us a far more exceeding and eternal weight of glory.
(2 Cor. 4:17 KJV)

This sentence in 2 Corinthians is dealing with spiritual and eternal issues, but the application to earthly and temporal issues is valid.

Rational Thinking Versus Irrational Thinking

In the late 1950s, Albert Ellis reintroduced (Proverbs and Paul said it first) a simple concept that could be called the ABCs of emotional reaction.

A = the activating event (triggering event)
B = the belief (what one thinks or says to oneself about A)
C = the consequence (the resulting feelings and behaviors)

The A (activating event) can be minor, such as dripping gravy on one's shirt or blouse. Or it can be major, as when a person's job is lost. The A by itself does not produce the C (consequence). One person might react to being fired (C) by becoming depressed, even suicidal. Another person may view being fired as a chance to change to a more desirable job. Clearly, A did not automatically produce C. It is our B (belief) about A that determines our response. Let's look at some couple interaction using the ABCs.

Earl gets a phone call from his wife, shortly after he arrives at work, thanking him for his support during yesterday's rough times. He feels good about the call all day. Putting Earl's situation in the ABC format looks like this.

A = phone call from his wife thanking him for all of his help.

B = Earl thinks to himself, *I guess I do have something to offer. It was nice she called. But I'm a pretty nice guy, too. And my advice isn't too bad.*

C = Earl feels happy. His behavior during the day is cheerful.

Andy is called into the kitchen by his wife who tells him that she appreciates his helping with dinner when she has to work late, but coming home to a messy kitchen takes much of the fun out of it. Andy is depressed, and is quiet and withdrawn for a day. Looking at his ABCs we see this.

A = Andy hears his wife say she appreciates his help but doesn't like the mess he leaves.

B = *I never do anything right. Everytime I try to help, it turns out badly. I've got a reverse King Midas touch; everything I touch turns to garbage. I'm not perfect, but I must be. I think the family would be better off without me. In order for me to be okay, I must be thoroughly appreciated. They don't appreciate me, therefore, I'm not okay.*

C = Andy feels worthless and depressed. For the next twenty-four hours he mopes around the house.

The ABCs are used by all of us, whether positively, as in Earl's case, or negatively, as in Andy's. There was a difference between Earl and Andy though, a difference that went beyond the positive and negative. In Earl's case, what he told himself at B was the truth. What Andy told himself at B was false. In Andy's case it is easy to see that his upset came more from what he told himself at B than what was told to him at A.

Albert Ellis proposes the concept of irrational beliefs. These beliefs are not irrational in the sense of crazy-out-of-control but in the sense of being false. He believes that humans are biologically prone (some much more than others) to think irrationally.

Look for the Musts, Look for the Shoulds

For Ellis, the chief characteristic of irrational thinking is the use of the absolute. The "I must," "ought," "should," or "have to" are common absolutes. Extremes in language, such as "always" and "never" are also evidence of irrational thinking. Regardless of the words used, there is a sense of demand. I demand something of myself or of others—not a preference, or even a strong preference, but a demand.

People who believe they must do or be something will be very upset if they do not live up to these demands. People who believe a spouse, or a child, or a driver of the other automobile must behave in a certain way will be very angry if the others do not live up to these demands. We teach our clients that it is healthy and rational to desire things. Desires, even strong desires, do not generally get us into difficulty. It is *demands* that cause us and others problems. We often use the following illustration:

The Swimming Pool Analogy

You are staying at a hotel. It is a hot August afternoon and you are sitting by the pool. You notice someone walking by with an ice cold lemonade and you decide you want one, too. You locate a lemonade stand a short distance from the pool, but just as you get there, the man in charge puts up a sign saying, Closed until 4 (it is now 3:25). "Please, can't you fix just one more before you go?" you ask. "Sorry," he says, "I don't have any more made up and it is time to recharge the chemicals for the pool. It's the state law. If you don't want to wait until I get back you can use the pool entrance to the coffee shop for a Coke."

What do you do? Beat the guy up because he won't give you a lemonade? Of course not. You only desired a lemonade. It was not a "must." Getting the lemonade was not a life-or-death situation. When you don't get what you desire you are disappointed. The stronger the unmet desire, the stronger the disappointment. Regardless of how disappointed you are, you can handle it. Like Paul, when you don't get what you desire you are cast down, but not destroyed. Let us return to poolside.

This time you are sitting on the edge of the pool at the deep end. You are carelessly playing with an expensive ring. It slips off your finger and drops into the pool. After several dives into the pool you locate the ring. It is wedged into the drain opening at the bottom of the pool. You take several deep breaths and dive in. Since the ring is wedged, it takes a few seconds to work it loose. You are almost out of air as you make your way to the surface. Someone with a morbid sense of humor has been watching the whole thing. As you are about to break the surface, this guy jumps into the pool and holds you under. You are running out of air. You struggle to get away. You can't. He persists on holding you under.

What do you do? This is not a mere desire for air—something like the lemonade that would be nice, but not necessary. This is vital! This is a life-and-death situation! This is not a desire situation, it is a demand situation.

When we ask our clients what they would do, they usually indicate that they would do something drastic. They would bite, kick, gouge—with intent to inflict harm. A demand condition merits extreme reaction.

With the swimming pool analogy clearly in mind, we now have a frame of reference, a yardstick against which life circumstances can be measured. You can ask yourself, "Is this a *desire* or a *demand* situation? Is this a postponed lemonade or a probable drowning?" It is easy to see how an irrational reaction becomes a rational one.

An extreme response to a demand situation and a mild-to-moderate response to a desire situation is rational. A mild-to-moderate response to a demand (life-or-death) situation is as unhealthy as the much more common demand response is to a desire situation. Let's examine a demand response to a desire situation.

Hugh, Lisa, and their three children are planning to leave Saturday morning on a camping trip. Lisa gets clothes ready for herself and the kids but doesn't pack Hugh's because she doesn't know what he wants to take. She gets the sleeping bags, tent, gas stove, and lantern out of storage, but isn't sure how Hugh wants them packed. Also, the tent is heavy for her. They are out of stove and lantern fuel but she figures they can pick up some stuff (fuel, gas for the car, ice, and some snack food items) on the way out of town.

Hugh has a somewhat different idea in mind. When he was a kid his family went camping a lot. His mom and the kids picked Dad up at work at four on Friday afternoons with the station wagon packed and gassed up, all the supplies aboard, ready to travel. Hugh is expecting a similar situation. He is planning to get up at seven, jump in the van, and be on the way to the trout stream by eight.

Lisa is planning to get up around eight for a vacation kind of breakfast, finish doing some last-minute chores, and be ready to leave the house by ten. By the time they make the necessary stops (in her plan) and drive to the campsite it would be about noon—time for her to prepare lunch.

We can see a potential crisis brewing. Lack of communication is the culprit. Let's suppose that Hugh comes home on Friday night at eight thirty. After Lisa's welcome-home kiss, she asks, "What are your plans for leaving tomorrow?" After hearing his plans, she gives hers. They use compromises and trade-offs. Lisa agrees to take the car tonight to the twenty-four-hour market and buy the fuel, ice, and groceries while Hugh loads the van. In the morning, he'll make breakfast while she packs what clothes he has laid out. They'll gas up on the way out.

The compromise isn't how either of them had planned it, and it involves adjustments, with some inconvenience for both. They each had viewed the situation as two people wanting two different things. When they discussed things on Friday night, there was no accusation or feeling that the other person was bad, wrong, selfish or irresponsible. Hugh and Lisa have learned to tell the difference between desire, what they would like, and demand, what they firmly believe they must have.

Many individuals and couples handle potential crises in ways that only compound the problem. Their miscommunication is the trigger or activating event, but the negative self-talk or irrational beliefs create the explosion. Now, consider the Hugh and Lisa story with a different twist, using the ABCs.

Beliefs or self-talk is often on two different levels: the more conscious level, in which we are aware of what we are saying, and the less conscious level, which is the implication of what we are telling ourselves. *The implied material in B will be in parentheses.*

Hugh arrives home at eight-thirty in the evening. After a kiss, Lisa asks, "What are your plans for leaving tomorrow?" After hearing his plans, she gives hers. Hugh's ABCs are as follow:

A = Lisa is not packed. She is not ready to go.

B = I can't believe she isn't packed. (*What she did was too far out of line to be believable or acceptable behavior.*) I work so hard for this family (*I contribute much more than Lisa does.*) What does she do with her time? (*She is irresponsible. She takes advantage of my generosity. She's on some kind of a free ride.*) My mom always was ready to go. (*Lisa must do things the way Mom did for Lisa to be acceptable as a person. She doesn't, and so she is not!*) Mom knew what Dad liked and did it. (*If Lisa really loved me, cared anything about me, or even respected me, she would have been packed. She wasn't packed. Therefore, I just do not matter to her.*) She always waits until the last minute to do things. (*Lack of organization and planning is a personal failing.*) I can't stand the way she messes up my life. (*Her behavior is completely objectionable. No sane person could bear it. She literally is driving me to insanity.*)

C = Feelings of rage, depression and, fear of losing control. Behavior includes yelling, swearing, and threatening to never take the family on another vacation.

Emotional Algebra

As you read Hugh's internal dialogue at "B" you see that the more destructive thoughts are at the lower level of consciousness. These are the thoughts that Hugh is not fully aware of unless they are pointed out to him. You might wonder how a counselor can suspect something is going on if it is outside the counselee's awareness. This is where the usefulness of "emotional algebra" comes in.

In the algebra problem $3 \times Y = 12$, we know that $Y = 4$. Even if we do not know anything about the rules of algebra, the answer can be figured out by trial and error. Y couldn't $= 1$. Three Ys would only be 3, so 1 would be too small. Likewise in emotional algebra, $A \times B = C$. In Hugh's case, his emotional algebra is A (minor incident) $\times$ B (unknown strength of the self-talk) $=$ C (major emotional and behavioral eruption). In order for C to be major when A is minor, B has to be major.

It takes training in cognitive behavior therapy and clinical experience to know what the irrationally thinking client is probably telling himself or herself. Understanding the emotional algebra concept, however, enables both the less experienced counselor and the client to figure out the probable content of B.

CHANGING THE BELIEFS

If the irrational beliefs cause the overreaction at C, then it makes sense that if B can be made less intense and more rational, C would become more appropriate and realistic.

Let's suppose that Hugh and Lisa had been in marriage counseling. One of the issues that had received attention was their tendency (Hugh to a greater degree, Lisa to a lesser degree) to exaggerate the importance of certain situations. Let's further assume the counselor had explained the ABCs to them. They had been trained to follow an emotionally explosive situation with a time-out. The time-out period was structured to allow twenty to thirty minutes away from each other—partially to cool down, and partially to collect their thoughts, and write out their ABCs. Hugh had followed the time-out procedure. After his blowup, he went to the basement and thought for a few minutes. Then he wrote out the ABCs.

When they had their next appointment with the pastor a few days later, they went over Hugh's ABCs. What Hugh had brought to counseling was only the Bs outside the parentheses, the self-talk he was consciously aware of. The counselor speaks:

> Well, Hugh, while I can see you were bothered by the blowup, it doesn't seem that your Bs were strong enough to create that big of a reaction. I think there are some hidden assumptions and implied beliefs we need to look for. I'm going to take each sentence you've written here and see if there aren't some things you were thinking that you were not aware of. This is going to be trial and error. I'll suggest things. If they fit we'll keep them in. If they don't, we'll discard them. Okay?

The counselor then added the statements contained in the parentheses.

> You know that your feelings about Lisa came from what you were believing. Our next step, then, is to analyze each sentence at B, both the ones you wrote at home and the ones we added in parentheses here. If they are truthful sentences we'll keep them; if not, we'll reword them so they are truthful.

Adding the D to the ABCs

The D stands for *disputing or debating*. This is what goes on when we look at our initial belief statements and ask, "is this true?" or, "where is the evidence that my belief is valid?" If the belief is valid, we leave it. If not, we change it.

We'll now look at what happens when Hugh and his counselor went over his Bs. The original statement is in regular type with the new or corrected B in **bold** type. The reason for the change is in *italics*.

> I can't believe she isn't packed!
> *Can't means impossible.*
> **I expected her to be packed.**

What she said was too far out of line to be believable and acceptable behavior.

The "too" in "too far" is an exaggeration—which literally means it just can't be that far. "Out of line" is a judgmental statement, implying that this behavior is totally, by any standards, socially unacceptable.

I didn't like finding she wasn't packed.

I work so hard for this family.

The "so" implies the degree of work was well above and beyond what is reasonable.

I work hard for this family.

I contribute much more to the family and marriage than Lisa does.

Is there evidence for this statement?

We both contribute to the family in our own ways.

What does she do with her time?

The question by itself is not irrational.

What does she do with her time?

She doesn't use her time wisely.

Does she always misuse her time? Do I ever?

Most of the time she is pretty productive with her time. She does have a different priority system from me when it comes to time.

She takes advantage of my generosity.

Is there any evidence to support this?

She is very thoughtful regarding our financial situation. I usually have to encourage her to spend on herself.

She's on some kind of a free ride.

Is there evidence to support this?

She has different values than I do but she does not take a free ride.

My mom was always ready to go.

Is there evidence to support this?

There were lots of times when Mom did all the packing for our trips.

Lisa must do things the way Mom did for Lisa to be acceptable as a person. She doesn't, and she isn't!
The "must" is absolute. Is this statement true?
I wish Lisa had some of Mom's traits, but she doesn't have to be Mom to be okay. In fact, I'm not too wild about some of Mom's traits.

Mom knew what Dad liked and did it.
Is there any evidence to support this?
Maybe Mom did what Dad liked about camping but not about everything.

If Lisa really loved me, etc., she would have been packed.
How does not packing prove she doesn't love me?
Lisa's packing for camping doesn't prove she loves me any more than not packing proves she doesn't love me.

She always waits until the last minute to do things.
Is this true?
Lisa does wait until the last minute on some things, but does others in a very timely fashion.

Lack of organization is a personal failing.
Does this mean she is a failure as a person?
I wish she were better organized, but she is a success in many other ways.

I can't stand the way she messes up my life.
Does she always or usually mess up my life?
Sometimes her way of doing things is a problem, but she adds much more than she detracts.

Her behavior is completely objectionable.
The word "completely" means totally and always.
Her behavior is sometimes objectionable, usually not. I'm sure that mine is objectionable to her.

No sane person could bear it. She is literally driving me to insanity.
How can her not packing make me insane?
No, she does not make me insane. If anyone makes me insane it is me. I don't always like the way she does things, but I don't have to make myself crazy over it.

If we look only at the bold type statements, Hugh's new **B** is this.

I expected her to be packed. I didn't like finding the van wasn't packed. I work hard for the family. We both contribute to the family in our own way. What does she do with her time? **Most of the time she is pretty productive with her time, although she has a different priority system than I do. She is very thoughtful regarding our financial situation. I usually have to encourage her to spend on herself. She has different values than I do, but she does not take a free ride.**

There were lots of times when Mom did all the packing for trips. **I wish Lisa had some of Mom's traits, but she doesn't have to be Mom.** In fact, there are some things about Mom I'm not too wild about. **Maybe Mom did what Dad liked about camping, but not about everything.**

Lisa's packing for camping doesn't prove she loves me any more than not packing proves she doesn't love me. Lisa does wait until the last minute for some things but not on others. I wish she were better organized, but she is a success in many other ways. Sometimes her way of doing things is a problem, **but she adds much more to my life than she detracts. Her behavior is sometimes objectionable, but usually not. My behavior, I'm sure, is sometimes objectionable to her. No, she does not make me insane. If anyone makes me insane, it's me. I don't always like the way she does things, but I don't have to drive myself crazy over it.**

Adding the E to the ABCDs

Hugh's new **B**s, his rational beliefs, produce a new effect, the **E**. The new effect changes the way he feels and behaves. The **E** is this: Hugh is disappointed with Lisa's behavior, but not because she is a bad, selfish, or lazy person. His disappointment is partially due to miscommunication and partially due to each of them having different priorities. She had organized her world differently than he had. With some nonjudgmental communication, it would have been possible through compromise and trade-offs to come to a conclusion that would have been satisfying to both of them.

We have presented exactly, not a summary, of how we help our clients change their irrational beliefs. Hugh's material may be tedious for some readers to go through, but this is exactly what goes on in therapy. Irrational statements are identified (B), challenged (D), and new beliefs and feelings (E) result.

COGNITIVE THERAPY RESOURCES

Several books are recommended to give the Christian counselor greater understanding of the cognitive behavioral arena. First, we suggest two books by Albert Ellis, the father of this theoretical position as we know it today: *Reason and Emotion in Psychotherapy* and *New Guide to Rational Living*.[1] The first title is for professional counselors, and the second is written for the layperson. Be forewarned that Ellis's personal philosophy is atheistic and he liberally uses profanity in his writing. Once you sort the wheat from the tare, his material can be very useful.

David Burns's book *Feeling Good* is comprehensive and has some useful sections on employing cognitive behavior therapy to treat depression and anger. We sometimes recommend that a client read the whole book, but we are more likely to suggest specific sections that are relevant to the client's specific problem.[2]

From the Christian perspective, there are two cognitive behavioral therapy books we keep on hand for clients. They are *Telling Yourself the Truth* by William Backus and Marie Chapian[3] and *Self-Talk: Key to Personal Growth* by David Stoop.[4] While these two books cover the same general concepts, the material is presented differently. Some clients identify with one more than the other, so we often ask them to read both.

Summary

While the thrust of this book is not on changing patterns of thinking, cognitive behavior modification is often an important force in marital therapy. This is true because the way we view or interpret events has a major effect on how we respond to what our spouse does or says to us. This chapter has described a way to evaluate a person's thinking patterns and has suggested one procedure for changing patterns that are irrational.

CHAPTER NINE

INTIMACY: LEAVING AND CLEAVING

Intimacy is at the highest level of the marital pyramid. The diagram on page 126 shows that, to reach the highest level, it is necessary to have successfully mastered the lower levels. Perfect mastery is not a requirement, however. Most of us have minor negative personality traits. We don't always practice the communication skills we know. Our conflict management techniques sometimes are forgotten during stressful times. Nevertheless, if we have mastered the basic ingredients of the lower levels, we can move on to intimacy. In counseling, we encourage a couple to move to intimacy as soon as the techniques for the lower levels of the pyramid are being practiced.

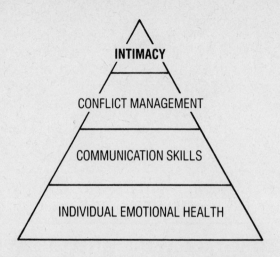

Fig. 9.1   The Fourth Level of the Pyramid: Intimacy

When working on personal psychological problems, communication breakdowns, or conflict issues, the focus is to try to eliminate the negative. Reducing the negative aspects certainly improves the marriage; however, that is not enough. If all the negative aspects in a marriage are gone, but there are no positive ones, the marriage becomes a marriage with no life, no excitement, and no joy. Thus, it is important to increase the positive aspects of a marriage. Building or creating intimacy is one of the best ways to do this. The thoughts, the feelings, and the behaviors of people in intimate relationships are positive: positive about the marriage, positive about their partners, and positive about themselves.

WHAT INTIMACY MEANS TO US

Counselors will be most effective in helping couples develop intimacy if they themselves experience it in their own marriages and are working on what intimacy means to them.

Harry Stack Sullivan's statement about love is a good starting place for discovering our meaning of intimacy:

> When the satisfaction, security and development of another person become as significant to you as your own satisfaction, security and development love exists.[1]

126

We believe this is what the Bible implies concerning marriage (see Ephesians 5). The kind of commitment Sullivan talks about can be made in a relationship where respect, trust, friendship, bonding, a healthy self-esteem, and a workable interrelating (communicating) style are in the process of being developed and refined.

We don't believe love and intimacy can be separated. We don't know if they can be equated, but they certainly go together. When partners are intimate, they are emotionally and physically close in a way that allows them to feel safe while being vulnerable. When talking about intimacy, the counselor might say the following:

> I can risk and you will not destroy me when I risk. Instead you will work with me in a way that allows me to be uniquely special and valued. It is safe both to agree and to disagree. I will be accepted. I can count on you and you can count on me.

The development and fostering of intimacy requires work. Much energy is put into developing closeness in a new relationship. However, in marriage, as time goes on, we somehow expect magic to take over and assume that we no longer must work at creating intimacy. There is no magic. Instead, we must work and spend time nurturing and fostering this growth of intimacy. This is especially true during the years in which we tend to take each other for granted.

We believe that discovering and developing certain behaviors that are nurturing and emotionally intimate is part of the process. For one couple we saw, it was important for the wife to be verbally reassured about joint decisions they had made earlier. This small act helped to create closeness. For the husband, a physical response such as a smile, a hug, or a love pat was a small behavior that was affirming and intimate. One of the rewards of being a counselor is the joy of seeing a husband and wife go from bewilderment to delight as they discover this intimate process.

It is important to note that the development of intimacy changes with the developmental growth and needs of the individuals involved. Therefore, this development is a process that changes over time. The end product is different as time goes on. Lastly, for us there is a strong connection between emotional intimacy and sexual intimacy. This will be further discussed in chapter 11.

DIFFERENCES OF INTIMACY

Our needs, understanding, and even capacity for intimacy grow and change as we grow and change. As counselors we look at intimacy as we look at most other relational issues— from the developmental perspective. This perspective considers the person's age when determining the appropriateness of the behavior.

It is certainly appropriate for a nine-month-old child to crawl. Crawling as the primary means of movement, however, indicates delayed development for the five-year-old. The same is true with intimacy. The feelings and behaviors described as intimacy for a couple during courtship may be appropriate and necessary for a courting couple. Yet, these same feelings and behaviors are unrealistic and inappropriate for a couple in their thirtieth year of marriage.

Normal physical growth moves through predictable, typical growth stages. There are times, though, when the existing physical behavior is not normal but is part of a pathological process. The same is true with intimacy. Some intimacy problems are developmental; that is, the person is just going through a stage. These problems resolve themselves in time. Other problems are not developmental and need therapeutic intervention to correct. The following sections describe basic human needs and fears and discuss typical developmental stages of intimacy. Following that is a discussion intended to help the reader gain understanding of intimacy that is problematic.

BASIC HUMAN NEEDS AND FEARS

As human beings we have many needs and fears, but two needs and two fears relate especially to our discussion. We need *closeness* and we need *autonomy*. Closeness implies connectedness and relatedness to another person. Autonomy implies individuality and independence from another human being.

We fear being abandoned as much as we fear being swallowed up or smothered. To be abandoned means to be isolated, to be left totally alone. To be swallowed up or smothered means to lose one's identity. Being controlled by another person also causes one to feel as if one's identity has been lost.

These fears and needs imply that a balance is necessary. The goal is to be close but not consumed by the other, to have independence but not to be abandoned, to have freedom and autonomy but not isolation. The search for the balance point propels a couple through the developmental stages.

STAGES OF INTIMACY

The Honeymoon Stage. This is the wonderful stage of togetherness and oneness that most couples go through. In its pure form, the man and woman want to spend all their time together and seem to have similar tastes, feelings, and desires. In this stage they perceive each other as being incredibly alike.

In this honeymoon relationship of oneness, the need for closeness is certainly met, and there is no fear of abandonment. However, there is something potentially destructive about this stage if it continues too long. After a while the fear of being swallowed up by the other surfaces.

The Separation and Individuation Stage. In this stage the persons emphasize their own identities. They no longer see everything alike; in fact, they may begin to emphasize their differences in taste, ideals, friends, ways of doing things, personality traits, values, activities, parenting styles, and even religious convictions.

In this stage each person pulls away from the other (separation) and each one emphasizes his or her individual identity (individuation). Here the need for autonomy is served and the fear of being swallowed up is tamed. The fear of abandonment, on the other hand, is fueled since the need for closeness is neglected.

This stage is as typical as the honeymoon stage. The couple can negotiate this successfully and move to the last stage. Transition through this section, however, is often rocky.

Many people have an idealized or "Hollywood" view of marriage. This view, quite similar to the honeymoon stage, holds that if we are truly in love we will want to spend all our time with the other person; we will want and see most things alike, be free of conflict, and always thrill to the other's touch. According to this unrealistic view, if we no longer feel this way we must have fallen out of love, or at least the relationship must have gone stale.

Unfortunately, many couples divorce when in this second stage. The chance of divorce increases significantly when one of the partners has an affair at this stage of development. Affairs—not one-night stands—having just recently begun, are still in the honeymoon stage. Emotional difficulties arise when a person is simultaneously in the separation-individuation stage with his or her spouse and in the honeymoon stage with a new lover.

Pastors and church counselors can educate couples about these stages during premarriage counseling. If the couples can be intellectually prepared, they can focus on the development tasks of this stage that are a necessary preparation for the third stage. They can realize that wanting to have greater separation, wanting to spend time in activities that do not include the other, does not mean love is gone. It means only that the pendulum has swung away from togetherness toward individuality. They know that this swing, if not carried too far, is often a necessary step to an eventual balance between the extremes of total togetherness and total separateness.

One variation of the second stage occurs when individuals separate and individuate at different times. This difference in timing often results from their personality and the kinds of relationships that existed in their family when they were children. If one person has a very dependent personality, he or she will be threatened when the partner begins to separate and individuate. Attempts to control through manipulation of guilt or helplessness are common with these couples.

Again, even if couples feel the need to separate and individuate at different times, if they are intellectually prepared for this stage, the transition will be eased.

The Interdependence Stage. The first stage can be described as dependence, the second as independence, and the last as interdependence. Interdependence means that each person can live and function independently from the other. While possible, it is not necessarily pleasurable or as beneficial to do so. The interdependence stage is the midpoint between the extremes of total togetherness or dependence and total separation or independence.

Pathologic Variations. A common destructive variation begins in the second stage as the couple slowly separates and individuates. Partially due to the pressures of earning a living, raising a family, or serving the needs of the church and the community, more and more time is invested in other activities. This couple doesn't expect the honeymoon stage to last or perhaps they really didn't have one. Problems arise because they don't know that there can be closeness and togetherness *and* separateness all at the same time. A much more likely position is that the couple continue to hope for intimacy, but they are continually taking care of the immediate needs rather than setting the relationship as a higher priority.

If the counselor can begin work with a couple when they still care for each other, much can be done to help. Fortunately, this is the most common situation of couples coming for counseling.

THE FOUR "MUSTS" FOR MARRIAGE

Therefore shall a man leave his father and his mother, and shall cleave unto his wife: and they shall be one flesh. And they were both naked, the man and his wife, and were not ashamed.   (Gen. 2:24–25 KJV)

Charles Swindoll, in his book *Strike the Original Match*, has extracted four "musts" from this passage.
. . . a man shall leave—*Severance*
. . . and shall cleave unto his wife—*Permanence*
. . . and they shall be one flesh—*Unity*
. . . and [they] were both naked and were not ashamed—
Intimacy
Intimacy cannot truly exist without the presence of the first three "musts": severance, permanence, and unity. We will deal with these briefly. While the labels are Swindoll's, what follows is by the present authors.

131

It could be inferred from the above that intimacy is connected with sexuality. Lest a reader misinterpret our meaning, we believe sexual behaviors and feelings are not synonymous with intimacy. While the most fulfilling sexual experience happens when the husband and wife are experiencing intimacy, it is also common for couples to engage in sexual intercourse without feelings of intimacy. Fortunately, a couple can experience high levels of intimacy without sexual behaviors being part of their experience. This, along with other related issues, will be discussed in the following chapter, "The Emotional-Physical Connection."

Severance. Leaving father and mother has great psychological importance. Early in our psychological development (usually in the first four years of life) we all went through a process of separation and individuation to become separate, unique individuals. We were separate, and yet we were not abandoned. We could leave, at first by going into the next room, and later by spending the weekend with grandma; when we came back Mom and Dad were still there. Or, Mom and/or Dad would go away, but they would come back. We learned we could switch from being alone to being together and back to being alone. We were not swallowed up and we were not abandoned. We had true closeness and we had true autonomy.

In adolescence many people go through new separation and individuation. This has to do, primarily, with values and beliefs. As children we believed all that we were taught. During the teen years come the questioning, the challenging, the rejecting and discarding, and, finally, the reclaiming and accepting of much (not all) of what we were taught. We create our individual version. Now our beliefs are ours, and we no longer are parroting our parents' beliefs. This process begins for many in early adolescence and continues, for the most part, until our thirties. (We never completely finish this task.)

A third separation and individuation takes place during adulthood when we physically (or at least symbolically) leave our parents. We move out of their sphere of direct influence. "When you live under my roof you'll do it my way," was probably first said by Adam. While this separation is important to a person's individual development, it is of even greater importance to the development of any intended marriage, for in such a relationship the allegiance is switched from parents to spouse. The command to "leave and cleave" appears in the Bible before the command to "honor and obey one's parents. One's spouse must know that he or she is the most important person to the other person. He or she also must know that, while one still loves one's parents, the spouse is in first place.

Spouses who are still tied to Mom and/or Dad have a genuine psychological problem. They may describe it as love or even quote the command to "honor thy father and mother," but the real issue is unresolved dependency. They have not separated and individuated enough to trust anyone but Mom or Dad. They are not, in any way, ready for marriage.

Permanence. God intends marriage to be permanent. Paul tells us, "To the married I give this command (not I, but the Lord): A wife must not separate from her husband. But if she does, she must remain unmarried or else be reconciled to her husband. And a husband must not divorce his wife" (1 Cor. 7:10, 11). Not only is permanence God's will for marriages but permanence provides emotional, physical, and financial security to the wife and husband.

Commitment is an aspect of permanence. Commitment is one of the factors that causes the marriage to endure. When things are going smoothly or when the couple is deeply in love, commitment is not needed to keep the couple together. It is when things are rocky or when little affection exists that commitment comes into play. Commitment is the glue that holds the couple together during those times the marriage has little going for it.

When we counsel someone who is sure the marriage is over, we use such models as Falling Out of Love—Falling Back in Love to encourage them.

Unity. In a healthy marriage, to be united means to share a common commitment, a common purpose, and common goals. It means agreement on the central issues. Unity is giving up some of myself. For the sake of the relationship, I put my spouse ahead of parents, friends, activities, and children. My spouse does likewise. This is unity.

The concept of unity can get distorted by an insecure or jealous spouse. This person not only wants to be placed before parents, friends, activities, and children but even resents those things getting second-place attention. When this problem occurs in a marriage we share the *number one versus number only* concept with the couple. Being *number one* means I'm first. My spouse puts me ahead of our parents, friends, activities, and even our children. I get my share. My spouse spends time with our parents, children, and friends, and in activities, but not to the detriment of our relationship.

Being *number only* means that there is nothing that my spouse does without me. I need all the time and attention my spouse has. Parents, children, friends, hobbies, and interests are not in second place. They are not even in the running. My spouse must be completely and totally mine and mine alone. Being number only is unrealistic and impossible.

As Christians, we are commanded to have no other gods before the Lord. In this century few of us are in danger of worshiping graven images, unless these be in the shape of BMWs, golf clubs, college diplomas, or even crosses. Did God say these things are sinful? They are not unless they are more important or come before the Lord. The same is true with one's spouse. Friends, children, jobs, hobbies, and parents are not wrong or bad. Each can have a place; and as long as that place is of less importance than the spouse, the person is being obedient to the principle that will give life to the couple and to their marriage.

Intimacy. We refer you back to our discussion of what intimacy means to us. We encourage counselors to think in broad terms. Intimacy is emotional as well as sexual. In most cases, the sexual intimacy in marriage is achieved only after the emotional work is attended to.

GRIST FOR THE MARRIAGE MILL

Another important aspect in moving toward intimacy, we believe, is the notion of "grist for the mill." Diana, a woman in her early thirties, comes into the office and says:

I know that I shouldn't be doing this, but it is wonderful. Bob and I can sit at a restaurant for hours, talking over a cup of coffee. We always have something to say. I can really communicate with him. That's one thing for sure my marriage doesn't have. I just can't communicate with my husband.

Diana believes she is in love with Bob. She has a feeling of closeness with him she doesn't have with her husband. What is going on both between Diana and Bob, and Diana and her husband?

Diana and Bob are sharing their history with each other. They are interested in finding out about the other and telling their own personal stories. This doesn't happen only in affairs; it happens also at the beginning of most relationships.

By contrast, Diana and her husband have stopped sharing. They know each other's personal history, so there is not much to discuss that is new in that area. More importantly, they have not developed other things to talk about.

If we examine long-standing or mature marriages we find that the partners have as their substance shared interests and activities. The couple spends time talking and planning their activities and projects. Then, as they enter their activities and work their projects, they spend time together. When the activity or project is history, they can remember it and live it again together. The time spent together is not just focused on the past, present, or future activity. But it is during this process that, naturally and spontaneously, other thoughts and feelings are disclosed. The sharing of these spontaneous thoughts and feelings increases the sense of closeness for the couple.

Intimacy is produced not by sharing our thoughts and feelings with each other as much as having them accepted by the other. So it is self-disclosure and the acceptance of that disclosure that produce intimacy.

The relationship or marriage mill needs something to grind if the relationship is to survive and grow. For a new relationship, the grist for the mill is sharing history. But that is usually temporary. If Diana is not careful she could leave her husband for Bob only to find in a couple of years that they had little to talk about. Since the grist for the mill in a successful marriage is sharing interests and activities (and the personal sharing that spontaneously occurs) she would be far better off bringing her husband into counseling. As they are taught to once again share their lives, interests, and activities with each other, her feelings of closeness for her husband can be rekindled.

This concept is important for premarriage as well as marriage. Sooner or later the couple runs out of personal history to share and something of a more lasting nature must take its place.

COUNSELING TO IMPROVE INTIMACY

Ralph and Veronica spent several minutes in one counseling session before they were able to express the main reason for their being there. Finally, Ralph said, "What we desire most is to be intimate. We don't seem to have intimacy in our marriage.

A little probing revealed that Ralph wanted a sexual relationship that was more exciting for both of them. But he maintained that something else was missing. The counselor decided that a starting point for working with them was to establish two things: What did intimacy mean to each of them, and how would they know when they had achieved it?

When asked to define intimacy beyond the sexual aspect, many couples will not be able to do this without some help from the counselor. We have discovered that what creates intimacy for one couple will not create intimacy for another. As discussed earlier, this will also vary according to where each person is in the life cycle. Newlyweds will describe it as the excitement of being together, while a couple married fifty years or more may describe intimacy as the very special way they think and anticipate events alike. One of the first tasks of the counselor is to discover the private and unique meaning of intimacy for each person and for each couple.

Handling the Time Factor

We have talked about this before, but it seems to be such a "sign of the times" we want to mention it again. More times than not when couples come for counseling, they are having difficulty with time. There are too many demands on their time. It often becomes necessary for you, the counselor, to contract with them in an assignment format, to create couple time. We have had couples bring their calendars to the counseling session and set up times to spend together. Basically, we help them make appointments to spend pleasurable time together. Couples may need your help to get started. Getting ahead financially, or with their careers, may be strong competition for time.

Forgiveness and Grace

Since none of us is perfect, there is always a need for forgiveness and grace. The Scriptures give us strong advice on the necessity of forgiving.

> Then the master called the servant. "You wicked servant," he said, "I canceled all that debt of yours because you begged me to. Shouldn't you have had mercy on your fellow servant just as I had on you?" In anger his master turned him over to the jailers until he should pay back all he owed. This is how my heavenly Father will treat each of you unless you forgive your brother from your heart.
>
> (Matt. 18:32–35)

> Do not judge, and you will not be judged. Do not condemn, and you will not be condemned. Forgive, and you will be forgiven. Give, and it will be given to you. A good measure, pressed down, shaken together and running over, will be poured into your lap. For with the measure you use, it will be measured to you.   (Luke 6:37–38)

These passages indicate that God's forgiving us is directly related to our forgiving others. There is an earthly application here as well as a heavenly one. Forgiveness begets forgiveness. If we forgive our brother (spouse, in this case) our brother will much more likely forgive us.

These commands to forgive enable us to be free to grow, and are not just to make the other person feel better. Lack of forgiveness creates walls of bitterness, resentment, anger, and depression. When this happens it becomes almost impossible to move forward in one's life. Forgiveness done in a loving, caring manner (grace) is based upon respect and unconditional love for the individual. This kind of forgiveness is not necessarily earned or deserved; nevertheless, it is given.

It is useful to share with counselees how forgiveness really works, since many people have misconceptions. Forgiveness begins with a decision to forgive. This decision is followed by acting in a forgiving way, performing actions that demonstrate forgiveness. Actual feelings of forgiveness may not come until much later. The process takes time and a person must repeat the process because old hurts emerge in new ways, from different sources, and at different times. When this happens, the individual will find it growth-producing to get back to the decision-making step: *decide, act in a forgiving way, and then experience the feeling.* When a person finds it no longer necessary to go through these steps consciously, he or she knows that the process has been successful.

It is useful also to work with counselees with regard to forgetting. As humans, we can't really forget because our minds were not designed to do so. But aren't we supposed to forgive and forget? We say no. Instead, what a person can do is put the hurtful event into a productive perspective. Then he or she can move ahead in the relationship.

For example, an unfaithful partner now wants to change things in the relationship, to create intimacy for both partners. But they are not able to shift the focus from the affair. Although they conclude they still love and respect each other and want the marriage to work, they do not know how to handle the affair and what to do with the hurt and resentment. Exploring the notion of forgiveness with a counselor gives them hope. They need to be able to talk about the process of forgiveness. Useful books on the subject are *Caring Enough to Forgive,* by David Augsburger, and *Forgive and Forget,* by Lewis Smedes.[2]

An Exercise for Sharing Feelings

Sharing feelings is part of intimacy. Finding the right words to describe a thing is difficult for many people. Larry Day has developed an exercise that is helpful in initiating the sharing of feelings.[3] The couple is given a list (found in Appendix 2) of words that express feelings. They are to choose one of these words to fill in the blank in this sentence stem: "I feel _____ when _____.

I feel *accepted* when *you smile at me.*
I feel *trusted* when *you ask my opinion.*

They are to spend a specified amount of time in this activity. Having the couple practice this in the office usually increases their success rate later.

Structured Dialogue

Where the feelings and behaviors of intimacy are lacking but the desire for intimacy is present, structured dialogue is an excellent tool. By this time in your counseling a couple knows, or at least they have heard you say (you may wish to say it again to be sure) that feelings lag behind behaviors. You have told them, "You'll have to continue a behavior change for a while before the feelings begin to catch up." Knowing this, the couple is ready to begin structured dialogue.

The purpose of structured dialogue is to bring about a sense of closeness or oneness through verbal sharing of experiences, ideas, desires, and feelings. In a satisfying communication between two friends, each shares what is in his or her heart and each listens to the other. I know what my friend thinks and feels about things, and my friend knows what I'm dealing with as well.

Is there any difference between engaging in structured dialogue and just visiting with one another? Yes, there is. Structured dialogue is programmed visiting. It is a useful tool when spontaneous visiting is not happening naturally. Obviously, when neither person is talking, friendly visiting and sharing is not taking place. Also, one person talking and the other listening (especially if this is a standard practice for the couple) is not dialogue; it is monologue.

While the word *dialogue* has its origins in ancient Greece, current-day movements and writers have added to it. The Marriage Encounter movement of today has refined and promoted the exercise, giving a couple a structured format to help develop the kind of communication that enhances intimacy.

In structured dialogue, each person spends a period of time (ten minutes) writing out his or her feelings about a selected topic (for example, having the family reunion at your house this year). Then they spend the same period of time together sharing what each has written, followed by a brief discussion of the information shared. This is called a 10/10: 10 minutes of individual time thinking and writing, and 10 minutes of joint time sharing. There is nothing magical about 10 minutes. It could be 15 or 20 minutes; then they would have a 15/15 or a 20/20. A good reason for the 10/10, however, is that the total time spent is 20 minutes, a manageable amount of time for most couples daily. A "10/10" can be practiced for the rest of their lives. Longer time periods, particularly when discussing more important, complicated, or sensitive issues, make sense, but regular use of a 30/30 would become burdensome.

In our counseling we have found that it is difficult to bring couples to the place of complying with a daily routine of 10/10. Using a 20/20 time period on Monday, Wednesday, and Friday, or a 30/30 on Tuesday and Thursday may work better for some couples. Once the time period, frequency, place, and the hour have been negotiated between the two partners, the counselor and the couple sign the agreement, to ensure compliance. Keeping the original and giving them a photocopy to tape to their refrigerator door may add a sense of importance to the process.

In *The Secret of Staying in Love,* John Powell makes a distinction between dialogue and discussion. He sees dialogue as the sharing of emotions and feelings. Discussion is the sharing of thoughts, values, plans or decisions. He believes that both dialogue and discussion are important, but that we need to emphasize dialogue. He says:

> There must be an emotional clearance (dialogue) between two involved partners in a love relationship before they can safely enter into a deliberation (discussion) about plans, choices, values. The assumption behind this distinction and priority given to dialogue is that the breakdown in human love and communication is always due to emotional problems.[4]

Once the couple understands the importance of dialogue and agrees to begin the process, we frequently run into another problem, at least with one of the partners. One says, "What do I talk about? My husband (or my wife) always has something on his mind and can talk for hours but I seldom have anything pressing." Fortunately, some additional ideas can be added to time-period structure of dialogue.

One approach is to have each person carry a 3 × 5 card and to write down any idea that might prove useful in a 10/10 session. We find that the more people do this the easier it becomes. Then, at the end of each 10/10, the topic or issue for the next 10/10 is agreed upon. It is good for the partners to switch responsibility for coming up with the topic. Reassure the couple that the topic does not have to be profound. If dialogue becomes a habit, the necessary profound issues will surface.

An even more structured dialogue uses some already prepared topics. Among the helpful resources for this, we point couples to the last twenty-six pages of John Powell's book, *The Secret of Staying in Love.* For a somewhat different approach that is equally useful for dialogue, we recommend the Pauls's material, "How and What We Explore," from *Do I Have to Give Up Me to Be Loved by You?*[5]

In counseling, we have assigned selected sections from both of these books. The primary purpose of using this material is to teach counselees the dialogue process. In addition, the content in these books usually taps into issues with which our couples are struggling.

Eventually, after the couple has developed the practice of frequent open sharing, we want them to be able to generate their own material. If this type of interchange is happening on a regular basis, doing the 10/10 is superfluous. But if pressures of life creep in and the couple is not communicating, then it is time to go back to the more mechanical 10/10.

ENHANCING MARITAL INTIMACY THROUGH FACILITATING COGNITIVE SELF-DISCLOSURE

The heading for this section comes from the title of a book by Edward Waring[6] and follows the section on dialogue because self-disclosure is the theme in both.

Waring, a psychiatrist, has spent over ten years examining the role of intimacy in marriage. He has found that:

1. Intimacy is the dimension that most determines satisfaction with relationships which endure over time.

2. The quantity and quality of intimacy between husband and wife constitute the single greatest determinant of family function.

3. Self-disclosure is the single factor which most influences a couple's level of intimacy.

4. Marital intimacy can be enhanced by facilitating cognitive disclosure.

His research studies which compared couples with problems versus those reporting no problems showed that self-disclosure contributed most to the achievement of intimacy. Also, the relationship between self-disclosure and intimacy was linear: the more self-disclosure, the more intimacy.

An interesting method of self-disclosure is discussed by Gary Smalley and John Trent in their book, *The Language of Love*. In it they describe how to build intimacy by communicating through "emotional word pictures."

An emotional word picture is a communication tool that uses a story or object to activate simultaneously the emotions and intellect of a person. In so doing, it causes the person to experience our words, not just hear them.[7]

Understanding Levels of Risk

To become intimate a person must become vulnerable. We must open ourselves up to others. If our history of making ourself vulnerable to our spouses has been positive we will most likely continue to do so in the future. It is easy to be vulnerable when we are sharing what our spouses would like to hear. But what if it is something that might not please our partners?

Bev and Bob have a history of disagreements over a number of issues; but a major one concerns Bob's behavior when he is with his dad. Bob's dad likes to wager on almost everything—who is going to win a ball game, election, Miss Universe contest, or who'll catch the most fish? And when Bob is with him, he bets too. Bev is not so concerned about the money. She is simply opposed in principle to gambling. She was a preacher's daughter and gambling was clearly off-limits behavior. Bob feels that as long as he is not taking food off the table or supporting the Mafia, it's no big deal.

Bev and Bob do love one another and are committed to building their marriage. They know that openness and vulnerability to one another are important aspects. They both have agreed to be more open and accepting. Bob has decided not to hide the fact that he bets on the ball games or bets a penny a point with his dad when they play cribbage. Our scene opens about 9:45 P.M. on a Saturday. Bob has just gotten home from spending an afternoon and evening with his dad.

Bev: Did you have a good time?

Bob: Yeah, great! We fished at the lake until about seven o'clock. Then we went to eat.

Bev: Where did you go?

Bob: We went to that little Italian place where Dad likes to go. After dinner we played a few hands of cribbage and then I took Pop home. Boy, am I full.

Bev: Bob, did you gamble with your dad?

Bob: Yes. I won thirty-seven cents tonight. I'm improving.

Bev: Bob, how can you do that? Look at what you are doing to your testimony. I hate it when you spend time with your dad.

Bob: I thought you had agreed that if I would be honest with you about what I think, feel, and do, you would be accepting of me.

Bev: Yes, but what you did was wrong!

What is Bob's probable reaction? We can tell you because we know. Bob decided that he could not be completely intimate with Bev even though he loved her. She was too critical about certain things. His only other option was to keep quiet, or even lie. What if it were handled this way?

Bob: Yes, I won thirty-seven cents tonight. I'm improving.

Bev: You know, Honey, gambling isn't my favorite thing. I am very pleased that you told me and told me in a straightforward way. I love you and want to know about you. I feel close to you when you don't shut me out.

Bob: Thanks for not climbing all over me. I feel close to you when I can share something I know you don't approve of.

Which is the better scenario? In which is the relationship enhanced? Consider this model that we often share with our clients:

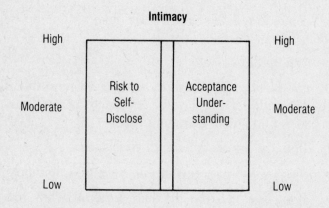

Intimacy

High		High
Moderate	Risk to Self-Disclose Acceptance Understanding	Moderate
Low		Low

Fig. 9.2   Self-Disclosure—Acceptance Model

In this diagram, intimacy is at the top. If a person risks a low level of self-disclosure ("Isn't this a beautiful day?") and the other person responds in kind ("It certainly is"), you feel okay— okay, but not intimate. A low-level risk and a low-level response equal low intimacy.

A risk that is at medium level for one person may be at a higher level for someone else. The interaction between Bob and Bev is somewhere between medium and high on the risk scale. In neither case did Bev approve of gambling. In the first scenario she did not respect or accept Bob as a person with rights. As a result, he decided the disclosure wasn't worth the risk. In the second scenario she still didn't like it. However, she could accept and respect him as a person, without judging or criticizing him, even though his behavior wasn't her first choice. There was a medium to high level of risk, and a medium to high level of acceptance and respect, and these resulted in a high level of intimacy.

Most good relationships spend much of the time at low and medium levels because there are usually not many high-risk issues. High-risk issues do appear from time to time, such as feelings about the partner's parents and siblings, issues concerning marital sex, finances, different parenting styles, and the revealing of an attraction to members of the opposite sex. These need equally high levels of acceptance and respect. The options are clear. If the risk is taken and acceptance given, a high level of intimacy results. If the risk is not taken or if the acceptance and respect are not given, intimacy will be denied.

Summary

Intimacy is at the top of the marital pyramid. It is the frosting on the cake and provides the greatest joy of a long-term marriage.

Intimacy is a process and moves through developmental stages. Understanding the psychodynamics that underlie each stage helps couples make the transitions from stage to stage.

Achieving intimacy is hard work. When the pressures of earning a living and parenting children, plus the demands of one's own self-development and fulfillment, all press in on a marriage, little energy is left over for the couple. Commitment—not just to stay married but to continually work on the marriage—is essential. Without effective dialogue true intimacy is not likely to be possible. In true dialogue, the partners' attitudes are open, accepting, nonjudgmental, and respectful.

CHAPTER TEN

INTIMACY: THE EMOTIONAL-PHYSICAL CONNECTION

The focus of this chapter is not on sexual problems and dysfunctions, or even sex education, but on the connection between sexual responsiveness and intimacy.

THE SEXUAL LADDER

In the early 1970s we attended a marital counseling workshop at the American Institute of Family Relations in Los Angeles where a staff psychologist, Dr. Mary Jane Hungerford, presented a concept that we have modified for our use. We call our version The Sexual Ladder.

A ladder has many rungs. There is no mystery about how to use a ladder; one starts at the bottom and climbs to the top.

Climbing a ladder is easy as long as it is done a step at a time. It is no harder to go from the ninth to the tenth rung than it is to go from the first to the second rung.

A ladder also describes how relationships develop. Most friendships start at what we call the lower end of the ladder—looking at each other, small talk, going for a walk. On the next page, The Sexual Ladder is displayed, showing these beginnings at the lower end. Most of the activities in the bottom half of the ladder are in the friendship bracket. A friend is someone with whom a person enjoys spending time. Feelings of affection develop out of friendship, but not with every friend. Friendship becomes courtship when both persons are available and have feelings of affection for one another. The relationship becomes more serious as the couple climbs the ladder into the affection area.

By the time most couples are engaged they are experiencing at least the bottom half of the sexual section of the ladder—"I

Fig. 10.1 Sexual Ladder

Love You," A Lingering Kiss, A Full Body Embrace, Nonbreast/ Nongenital Touch, and French Kissing.

A wonderful thing about courtship is that both men and women enjoy each rung of the ladder. Oh sure, a lingering kiss may be more fun than going for a walk. But going for a walk is still fun. Couples, after they are married, forget this and need to be reminded.

Look at the ladder for a minute and think about what a ladder is for. It is for getting to the top. And what is at the top of The Sexual Ladder? Sexual intercourse! This is a very common attitude among men. The top of the ladder is where "the good stuff" is while the bottom of the ladder is the stuff you have to go through to get to the good stuff.

Many Christian men resist getting to the top of the ladder during courtship because of their moral convictions. When they get married things often change. They think, "Sex is now legal. The top of the ladder is permissible. Paul even says it is wrong to avoid it. Boy, oh, boy! What luck!"

There are eighteen rungs on this ladder. During courtship many couples focus on the first fifteen. Once the "I dos" have been said, for the male, the focus is on the top three. Those are great—for a while anyway. However, sex can get too mechanical, too hurried, too centered on orgasm. After a time, concentrated focus on the three top rungs can actually cause sex to lose its intimacy. At this point couples often begin to experience problems.

Sex and affection go hand in hand. The goal for counseling is to help couples understand this connection.

KINDS OF LOVE

The Greeks describe four kinds of love: *eros, phileo, agape,* and *storge (STOR-GAY).* *Agape* (sacrificial love) and *storge* (commitment) come into existence by choice, whereas *eros* (sexual) and *phileo* (friendship) are emotional in nature. Choice and behavior do affect *eros* and *phileo*, but their roots are emotional. *Eros* is fueled by sexual desire and sexual attraction. *Phileo* is fueled by feelings of friendship and companionship. Both of these, along with *agape* and *storge*, are necessary for a happy, healthy marriage. Let's look at the role *eros* and *phileo* play in the overall courtship process.

The man is attracted to the woman because she is sexually appealing (*eros*). In addition, she might be the pastor's daughter, have a 4.0 grade-point average, be the captain of the volleyball team, be a champion debater, speak fluent French, run a six-minute mile, or have any other trait(s) the man finds attractive. Regardless of the attractiveness of these positive traits, he is attracted to her primarily in a sexual way.

The woman likes the man. She feels good around him. They talk about interesting things. They share many similar ideas. He seems accepting and supportive. He also just happens to be kind of a good-looking hunk. But even though he's good-looking, she doesn't think of him in terms of sexual intercourse.

During the courtship process the man begins to see more and more of the woman's nonsexual side. He finally comes to see her as a whole person. Yes, she is still sexually appealing, but there is much more to his attraction now. The woman finds that as their relationship grows she is thinking and feeling more and more often in sexual terms. As their friendship deepens, her physical desire for him emerges. The man starts at *eros* and if the relationship continues and everything else is satisfactory, he moves to *phileo*. For the woman the process is reversed.

This diagram has proved helpful to our clients. We often ask both male and female clients what there is about courtship that causes the woman to develop the *eros* side of her self? (The couple has already been shown The Sexual Ladder; they often

	Man	Woman
Eros	1	2
Phileo	2	1

Fig. 10.2   Male—Female Love Pattern

come up with the right answer.) The answer is that during courtship the man spends a great deal of his time (their time, really) at the bottom half of the ladder, in the friendship and affection range. The woman feels that she has a friend. For example, a couple has been dating for three or four months. On a Friday-night date, he asks her out a week or so ahead of time, giving her all week to think about it. Having a date set up gives him courage or permission to call her several times during the week. She loves the attention. When he comes to pick her up she can tell he has spent hours on his car just to impress her. He also looks and smells as if he's spent hours on himself. Again, to impress her. He is attentive, considerate, and complimentary in a genuine manner. Does she have sexual feelings when they sit close and talk? Sure she does.

Contrast the courtship to married life. It is now six or eight months after the wedding. They have both been working hard in their jobs. The long hours away from home, plus the chores at home don't leave much time to be together. Lovemaking is usually at the end of the day just before going to sleep. The approach to sex is a few kisses, some fondling, and then intercourse. As long as the wife appears to be excited about sex and eager to make love, the husband can be content.

However, the female partner in most couples we see (whose history is similar to what we have just described) is not excited about sex and eager to make love. In the physiological-emotional make-up of most women, *phileo* (friendship love) must be nurtured in order for *eros* (sexual love) to be fully developed. This is not so true with men. (We do find some reversal as people age. Men become more interested in the friendship factor and find *phileo* more and more rewarding. Women may feel sexual desires even in the absence of much *phileo*. With older people it is probably more accurate to say that both *eros* and *phileo* are important to both genders.) The old saying that men tolerate relationships to have sex and that women tolerate sex to have relationships is only partly true. We want our couples to enjoy both.

If sexual desire has left the marriage, we strongly encourage the couple to resume courtship, not for a few days, but incorporated as a permanent part of the marriage. We ask them to take the ladder and lay it on its side. What do we have now? It is not a hierarchy with sexual intercourse at the top, but a list of various options all at the same level. "Going for a Walk," "Sharing Dreams," "A Lingering Kiss," and "Sexual Intercourse" are all at the same level. These are different, yes, but equally important to the nurturing of the love relationship.

We ask couples to recall how enjoyable these activities were during courtship. By viewing each of these behaviors as valuable and enjoyable in its own right, rather than as a means to an end, both *phileo* and *eros* can return to the marriage.

The Sexual Ladder and the Male-Female Love Pattern diagram are useful counseling tools to help describe some of the problems the couple may have in the sexual area. Knowing what is wrong and how to correct it are necessary steps in the helping process. However, if the process stops here, improvement may not occur. The ideas need to be put into action. By assigning some specific behaviors and then telling the couple their progress will be checked next week may help do that. You might say something like this:

Clark, Rachel has said that it means a lot to her to receive a call from you during the day. You said you could do that, but you forget during the rush of the day. Here is a red label you can put on your phone. Whenever you see the label, ask yourself, "Have I called Rachel today." Before long the daily call will be a habit.

Rachel, I heard Clark say he liked it when you put on fresh make-up just before he comes home in the evening. Why don't you set the alarm on your kitchen clock-radio for fifteen minutes before Clark arrives. Now, next week I'll ask how your assignments went.

Summary

The key to fulfilling marital sexuality is to keep courtship in the marriage. Friendship and companionship and romantic sexual love are needed. The strong feelings of sexual desire are fueled by the gentler feelings of friendship. If the courtship behaviors are nurtured, which are much more in the "friendship" classification than sexual desire, sexual desire will remain strong.

CHAPTER ELEVEN

CONFIDENTIALITY IN MARRIAGE COUNSELING

Rich was angry. He questioned the pastor-counselor's good faith. He and Peggy had been in counseling for three months—supposedly working on their marriage. However, during all this time, Peggy had been seeing another man. Peggy knew what was going on, and so did the pastor. Rich didn't—he felt betrayed by both his pastor and his wife.

All the rules and ethics of counseling and confidentiality apply to marriage counseling. The pastor had honored his standard of confidentiality with Peggy. But he had obviously not given enough consideration to the fact that in marriage counseling there are three "clients"—the wife, the husband, and the couple.

In the above illustration the problem occurred because a secret was kept from one party. It can as easily occur due to counselor empathy. When we counsel, we attend closely to the client. Our attentive listening, eye contact, head nodding, clarifying questions, summary statements, and concerned tone of voice communicate that we care about our client. However, the client may misread our signals, confusing our empathy with agreement.

A typical situation of this kind occurs when one or both persons feel they need individual sessions. One may fear that complete honesty would upset his or her partner.

As mental-health professionals, we believe in unconscious defense mechanisms. We believe that people (some a great deal more than others) unconsciously present themselves in the best light. When remembering events, small details that may not support their position are not always recalled. The sequence of how things happened may be altered slightly. We know this happens with our clients, and with us.

After several sessions of empathic listening to an individual, it is very easy to convey to that person that you agree with him or her. If you are meeting with his or her spouse on an individual basis, each one will undoubtedly adopt this opinion to some degree. If one partner feels you favor one position much more than the other, you have allowed yourself, unwittingly perhaps, to be drawn into a power struggle. Furthermore, if the partners compare notes, which they eventually will do, they may feel betrayed by you. They may think you have lied, at least to one, and maybe to both of them.

If, at the very beginning of counseling with Rich and Peggy, the counselor had said, "While I'll see you individually from time to time, everything one of you tells me may be shared in our joint sessions," this difficulty would not have arisen. Either Peggy would not have shared her affair or Rich would have known about it in the next session. Either way, Rich's hurt and anger would not have been directed at the counselor.

Many marriage counselors prefer this approach because the counselor doesn't have to remember what can be shared and what can't. More importantly, the counselor will avoid the accusation that he or she has sided with one partner.

"Couples Only" in Marriage Counseling

The problem may be avoided in another way. The counselor could refuse to see either person individually. You could say, "Marriage counseling is couple counseling. If you want individual work, I'll refer you to someone else. When you see me, however, you need to come together." In this situation the counselor never knows anything the less-informed partner doesn't know. This and the previous approach are similar because they emphasize sharing of all information.

The marriage counseling field is divided on this issue. A larger percentage of professionals believe that individual issues as well as marital issues need addressing, and that the most effective way for this to happen is for the counselor to work on both an individual and a couple basis. If this path is chosen, the counselor might say the following to the prospective couple:

> I'd like you to be open and honest with each other. I prefer most, or even all, of our counseling to be in joint sessions. If you have a need to speak privately, we can meet individually. Eventually, I hope what is said in individual sessions will be dealt with in joint sessions. If, however, you have something you don't want to share with your spouse, I will keep that confidence. Do you both agree not to ask me what the other has said in individual sessions?

The way you choose is up to you. There is professional support for either of the alternatives. The most important thing to remember is that you must make very clear at the beginning what your limits of confidentiality are. The clients should then agree to work with you on that basis.

Professional Confidentiality

Whichever approach you choose—couples only or individuals and couples—you need to follow some formal ethical guidelines concerning confidentiality. The best approach is to belong to a professional counseling group; for those counseling in the United States, there are organizations such as the American Association of Pastoral Counselors, the American Association of

Marriage and Family Therapists, the American Association for Counseling and Development, and the American Psychological Association. Each of these groups has guidelines concerning confidentiality. For counselors in Canada, Europe, and in other parts of the world, it is hoped that similar groups exist.

The confidentiality section found in the Code of Ethics (1981) of the American Association of Pastoral Counselors is a good one to follow even if you are not a member of the organization.

PRINCIPLE III—Client Relationship and Confidentiality

Pastoral counselors respect the integrity and protect the welfare of persons or group with whom they are working, and have an obligation to safeguard information about them that has been obtained in the course of the counseling process.

A. It is the duty of pastoral counselors, during the counseling process, to maintain the relationship with the client on a professional basis.

B. Pastoral counselors do not make unrealistic promises regarding the counseling process or its outcome.

C. Pastoral counselors recognize that the religious convictions of a client have powerful emotional and volitional significance and therefore are approached with care and sensitivity. They recognize that their influence may be considerable, and therefore avoid any possible imposition of their own theology on clients.

D. Pastoral counselors do not engage in sexual misconduct with their clients.

E. Except by written permission, all communications from clients are treated with professional confidence. When clients are referred to in a publication, their identity is thoroughly disguised and the report shall so state.

F. Ethical concern for the integrity and welfare of the person or group applies to supervisory and training relationships. These relationships are maintained on a professional and confidential basis. Personal therapy will not be provided by one's current supervisor or administrator.[1]

Many professional mental-health groups model their guidelines upon those set forth by the American Psychological Association. Therefore, we have presented these below as printed in the *American Psychologist.*[2]

Principle 5
Confidentiality

Psychologists have a primary obligation to respect the confidentiality of information obtained from persons in the course of their work as psychologists. They reveal such information to others only with the consent of the person or the person's legal representative, except in those unusual circumstances in which not to do so would result in clear danger to the person or others. Where appropriate, psychologists inform their clients of the legal limits of confidentiality.

a.   Information obtained in clinical or consulting relationships, or evaluative data concerning children, students, employees, and others, is discussed only for professional purposes and only with persons clearly concerned with the case. Written and oral reports present only data germane to the purposes of the evaluation, and every effort is made to avoid undue invasion of privacy.

b.   Psychologists who present personal information obtained during the course of professional work in writings, lectures, or other public forums either obtain adequate prior consent to do so or adequately disguise all identifying information.

c.   Psychologists make provisions for maintaining confidentiality in the storage and disposal of records.

d.   When working with minors or other persons who are unable to give voluntary, informed consent, psychologists take special care to protect these persons' best interests.

We have discussed the legal and ethical issues of confidentiality. There is a practical reason as well. If you maintain strict confidentiality, word of this will get around. People will know that what is said to you in counseling is completely safe. Your opportunity to be of service increases when your reputation inspires trust.

Summary

Confidentiality is essential for successful counseling and it is a key element in establishing trust. Stating that what is said will be held in strict confidence helps build rapport. Not only is confidentiality a good professional practice; it is the law for credentialed professionals.

CHAPTER TWELVE

WHEN TO REFER

Guidelines for referring are frequently contained in the final chapter of counseling books. Such placement may cause the reader to infer that a referral is made when all else fails. We are placing this chapter earlier because we believe that referring needs to be kept in mind from the very beginning of counseling.

The counselor, after careful thought about his or her guidelines for referral, will want to explain them in ways appropriate to the counselee. If this person knows from the very beginning that a referral might be made, potential feelings of abandonment or rejection are significantly lessened. Before the "when to refer" question can be answered, however, the "why to refer" needs to be addressed.

WHY CAN'T THE COUNSELOR DO EVERYTHING?

Time limitations. Many pastoral counselors do not have enough time to see everyone who wants counseling, for as many sessions as some people would like. The counselor may need to establish some rules concerning who will be seen in counseling and for how many sessions.

The issue of who will be seen has been handled professionally and ethically in several ways. Part of the decision depends on the resources available and part on the philosophy of the church—assuming that a pastor is doing the counseling as a part of the church's ministry. Some churches have decided that counseling resources need to be "spent" on the members and regular visitors only. Other churches believe the counseling service to be an excellent outreach and that it should be available to anyone. Still other churches might prioritize the resources as follows: members and regular attenders, first; nonattendees not affiliated with another church, second; and nonattendees affiliated with another church, last.

Limiting the number of sessions is another way to fit the workload into the time available. Counselors in secular settings have found that setting a specific number of sessions is an effective way to manage a heavy caseload. If you and your counselees know you only have a fixed number of sessions (we recommend at least five) more work may get done. You have a greater justification to require written assignments to identify problem areas and review history. Later sessions can be spread over time.

Sally and Jim, we've only talked about thirty minutes, but from what you've told me I'm really optimistic about your marriage. I can already see where a number of positive changes can be made. First, we need to take care of some housekeeping details. Because of the number of people seeking counseling at our church, the Board has limited the number of sessions to ten. We may not need that many but let's plan in that direction.

For the rest of this session and next week's session, let's focus on defining the problem and looking at history. The third and fourth sessions, two and three weeks from now, will focus on communication. We will then switch to every other week for two sessions on conflict management and problem solving and two sessions on building intimacy. The last two sessions will be three and four weeks apart respectively. These will deal with maintenance and follow-up. So, while we only have ten sessions this plan spreads over nineteen weeks. It's my experience we can get a lot done in that time. It is also my experience that when we are finished we may not have followed this exactly. Let's get back to work now. Sally, why don't you share your feelings about Jim's family as he did about yours.

Possibly we should have titled this chapter "Methods to Avoid Referring" since we have just indicated how to work with a couple when the board has put time constraints on the counselor. If, as sometime happens, Sally and Jim turn out not to be the routine couple you originally imagined, referral is the next step.

It has been a month since we last met; and even though things are much better than when we started there is a way to go. As you know, we are limited to ten sessions. Since our last session I've been giving alternatives some heavy consideration. Both of you seem bogged down in anger and resentment. I feel that area needs some work. A good Christian psychologist, Dr. _____, is really expert in working with anger. I'd like to refer you to him.

Since the limitations of therapy were established in the very first session, this referral doesn't make you sound rejecting and the clients should not feel like failures.

There may be other conditions, especially if you are limited to three to five sessions in which you will arrange the referral within the first session. You may see that the problem is too complicated to work through in a few sessions. Or, you may work with only one facet—communication, for example—and then refer all other issues.

In real life, these ideas may not work as smoothly as laid out here. You may find yourself bending the rules and seeing the couple a session or two longer to ensure greater long-term benefit. In regard to referring, even though you have mentioned the possibility of referral early in counseling you may encounter resistance when the time comes. While the counseling and/or referring process may not go exactly as planned, we find that with specific and early structuring you will encounter fewer problems later.

Expertise limitations. All therapists need to be aware of their limitations. Some limitations are due to lack of training. Not all marital therapists are qualified sex therapists. Depression or phobias may be part of the marital problem and yet not all marital therapists are trained in these areas. All nonphysicians will eventually work with a couple in which one of the partners would benefit from some form of medication.

Not every counselee-counselor match-up is compatible. Sometimes incompatibility results from conflicting values. At other times, personality traits conflict. The most therapeutic and loving action you can take when you feel at odds with your counselees is to refer them to someone else. Pastors often believe they must support any termination of counseling or referral with strong evidence. In this kind of referral you don't have to sell the client on the validity of your position. Your own heart, gut feeling, or intuition tells you this is not going to be a therapeutic alliance. If you need a reason to refer, the following may provide a guide:

We've worked together for several sessions now and we don't seem to be making much progress. From my experience in matters like this I feel we are not connecting. I'm not hearing the problem in the way it is really affecting you and, therefore, I'm unable to get you excited, optimistic, or hopeful. I can't give you any tools that make sense. If we continue to work, I see our frustration increasing. I want you to continue counseling while you have some momentum. But I want you to do it with someone who can better help you. Before you go, I'll give you three names. You may find it beneficial to talk briefly with each one before you decide on the one with whom you will counsel.

Emotional entanglements. There are times when you can become emotionally entangled with a counselee. We all have weak spots in our psychological make-ups. If the weakness is minor, any disruption to the counseling process is minor. The major weak spots are the ones that cause problems. There are times when the issue rests primarily with the counselee; other times it rests with the counselor; and sometimes it rests with both.

It is a common occurrence for counselees to become overly dependent upon their counselors. Usually, dependent individuals can be successfully counseled if you set limits, such as not making decisions for them, ending the counseling session on time, not squeezing in extra counseling sessions, and not allowing other than emergency telephone calls between sessions. Dependency becomes a problem if you have a need to be needed. You may believe that by going out of your way to meet their needs, you are doing the right thing, but this is usually not the case. If you find yourself over-invested in a person, it is time to refer.

A counselor's feelings of anger or sexual arousal toward a client will render counseling more of a hurt than a help. Also, a strong need to protect or rescue clients, or a need to gain their approval, can impede counseling.

If these signs of emotional entanglement appear, you have two ethical choices: seek personal psychotherapy to resolve the issues or refer the client. If the problem occurs frequently, your own psychotherapy is the clear choice.

What do I tell the client? you may be thinking. A simple explanation is best. An appropriate response could be, "Most of us have some unfinished psychological business to do. We are not aware of it until someone accidentally touches that hidden area of our life. There is something about our relationship that triggers a response in me, causing me to lose objectivity, and this is getting in the way of your progress. Neither of us is at fault. It is not something you did wrong. However, I believe it is in your best interest if I help you link with another counselor."

THE PASTORAL COUNSELOR'S PERSONAL GROWTH

From time to time there are reports of counselors, even pastoral counselors, becoming intimately involved with their counselees. Counseling relationships are intense and produce levels of intimacy that can lead to temptation. But temptation can be avoided by keeping one's own personal house in order and by referring friends and close associates before counseling is begun. One of the best ways for pastoral counselors to minimize their becoming overly involved with the people whom they counsel is for the counselors to deal with their own personal growth, and the growth within their own marriage relationships. Life is a process of discovering how to make these relationships work. Counselors must put energy into making their relationships work, whether the relationship be with a spouse, a best friend, or a professional. Other things can get in the way of doing this personal care-taking. Counselors, like every other human being, are vulnerable.

Loneliness may also contribute to vulnerability. Pastoral counselors may be isolated from other professionals because they are the only ones doing the counseling in their churches. It is a good idea to maintain consistent contact with other professionals. Joining a local Christian Association for Psychological Studies (CAPS) chapter is one way of meeting that need.

CHOICES IN REFERRALS

Complete Referral

In the complete referral, the entire case is given to another professional. A referral of this type can be made for several reasons. A major reason may be lack experience or training with a specific problem. Although you may care about the couple, you relinquish your involvement with them in a counseling capacity. It is important for them to establish a therapeutic alliance with the new therapist and break off the one they had with you. After you have referred the counselees, calling them in for a status report is not appropriate; however, supportive contacts are. A supportive contact would be a written note or a verbal comment: "I'm thinking about you and praying for you. I hope things are going well."

Collaborative Referral

A collaborative referral is useful when you plan to be the primary marital counselor but you see some issues that need addressing that are out of your area of expertise. A physician might be used to treat depression, or evaluate impotence, or deal with premenstrual syndrome. A psychologist might be used to do a thorough personal assessment with a couple who has had several marriage counseling failures. There are noncounseling issues as well. You might refer to an estate planner, someone good with budgeting or time management, or an expert in elder care.

The collaborative referral could occur after your first interview, as a prerequisite to your planning treatment. You may need psychological or psychiatric evaluation in some cases before you can decide if you should work with the couple. The psychological or psychiatric evaluation could indicate that one or both partners need individual therapy before work can proceed on the marriage.

Summary

Referral belongs in the counselor's tool kit as much as empathy or diagnostic ability. Referral is not a sign of weakness but a sign of good judgment. It is a great relief to realize there are many cases you don't have to handle alone. And (even more relief) there are some clients you don't have to handle at all!

CHAPTER THIRTEEN

AN OUNCE OF PREVENTION

This chapter is dedicated to married Christians, be they counselees or the ones doing the counseling. If a marriage has problems we recommend professional help. For the strong marriage
we suggest a preventive maintenance program. Hopefully, the
following ideas will be of help.

"An ounce of prevention is worth a pound of cure" has great
relevance to marriage.

A sign at a local garage says, "Pay me a little now or pay me a
lot later." Most couples come to us hoping for cures. They are
paying a lot later—not only in the expense of marriage counseling, but also in the emotional cost of a troubled marriage.

Perhaps we could decrease the frequency of troubled marriages by applying some preventive strategies.

It takes little effort to keep an automobile in good running condition, and yet a lot of people ultimately have problems because of poor maintenance practices. Is this not also true for marriage? Many couples have read books or magazine articles or attended family-life seminars, and yet do not practice what they have learned. Why is this so? Let's explore some causes and some possible solutions.

IT'S EASY TO PROCRASTINATE

Out of sight, out of mind is the cause of many failures, mechanical and marital. Under normal conditions oil should be changed every three thousand miles. Hoses and belts begin to leak and break after four years of use. The prudent owner changes the oil every three thousand miles and the hoses and belts every four years. Many people don't, however. Their cars seems to run as well with oil that is four thousand miles old as it does with new oil. "What is this four-year stuff?" asks an owner. "I've had my car eight years and haven't changed a hose or belt yet." In a summer traffic jam, whose radiator is most likely to boil over?

Having a smoothly running car and a healthy marriage requires action. Both take time, and both won't happen by themselves.

The first step in achieving a healthy marriage is to establish the marriage as the top priority. As we said in the first chapter on intimacy, you and your spouse do not have to be "number— that is, *everything* to one another—only" but you do need to be "number one" for each other.

The second step is to determine a healthy and practical maintenance schedule for your marriage. You have general directives for maintenance of the marriage in the Scriptures; the Bible gives an outline regarding priorities and how you are to treat one another. However, the Bible does not give specifics for your marriage. You and your mate would do well to spend a weekend discussing the things that the other does that make you feel special.

Take a look at the suggestions in the intimacy section. The 10/10 dialogue (nearly daily) and the 30/30 dialogue (once a week) are like changing the oil in the car. We recommend a weekly inexpensive date with just the two of you. Once a month we would like you to be more extravagant. Dress up, look nice for each other, and go to a nice place. A weekend away at least every three months (more often if you can arrange it) is a tonic for your marriage. Remember and use the concept of courtship described in the chapter on the physical-emotional connection.

One complaint we often hear is, *we can't afford to do these things*. Remember the auto repair sign, "Pay me a little now or pay me a lot later." You can't afford *not* to.

Another justification for not spending time alone as a couple is, *the children don't like it when we do things by ourselves*. Or sometimes it's worded this way: "We believe in a strong family and we want to do things as a family." We are in favor of strong families, too. However, the foundation for the family is the husband-wife relationship. Parents can give no better gift to their children than their own strong marriage. If you had ten hours to divide, we believe your children would profit more from Mom and Dad spending five hours just with each other and five hours with the kids, than if all ten were spent with the entire family.

The third step is to religiously carry out your plan. Flexibility is fine. If I change my oil at 2,800 miles one time and 3,400 miles the next, probably I'm doing as much good as slavishly changing at 3,000 miles. Being a free spirit, however, doesn't entitle me to stretch the 3,000 to 5,000. If you can't meet a couple date, scheduling the next available time for the couple is essential.

It won't happen to me is another reason given for not being careful about "couple time." This is clearly foolhardy. It is like the adolescent who believes he is going to live forever. Since he can't conceptualize ever being dead, driving his motorcycle at high speeds without a helmet doesn't seem all that risky. "I've done it lots of times. No problem. Don't worry about me, Mom!" is his theme. We know better.

No machine is immune to friction and poor lubrication. No marriage is immune to the lack of loving maintenance. It is only pride that leads one to believe he or she is above the laws of nature and relationships.

The only way to deal with the idea of "it won't happen to me" is to accept the fact that it won't—as long as you engage in preventive maintenance.

I know things are out of balance but we'll get back on track when the crisis is past is a common refrain. This is the most plausible of the reasons, and therefore, for some couples, becomes the most dangerous. The lives of most professionals get out of balance while going through graduate training. We know that from personal experience. The writing of this book also threw our lives off balance. Maintaining two full practices and trying to keep up with family obligations and church responsibilities meant that we had to give up something, and the something was our recreational and leisure time together. Is this bad? For the short term, no, but for the long term, definitely, yes!

For the short term, people can go without vitamin C with little concern of harm done. But long-term deprivation produces scurvy. Marital scurvy (divorce) just isn't worth being careless about routine marriage maintenance.

Has anyone ever accused you of being too mature? One of the definitions of maturity is the ability to delay gratification? That is a problem with many Christians, especially with pastors and their spouses (we suspect). They can delay gratification, literally, until the kingdom comes. But divorce often occurs before God's kingdom comes.

The first step in the solution is to realize how a short-term solution can belie an underlying problem or could lead to a future problem. For example, a pastor may tell his wife, "We'll really put our nose to the grindstone while we are in the new building program. When we get into the new facility we'll organize our life more reasonably so that we have time for us." If the example could fit you, ask yourself, does the program, person, or church really need your participation at that level in order to function. If the answer is no, you may have a worth-through-works problem.

The worth-through-works belief system is never satisfied by your good efforts. You never do enough to feel free to enjoy leisure time with your spouse and yourself. Personal psychotherapy may be useful.

If the answer is yes, both you and your spouse need to agree that this is a worthwhile venture, but that neither of you will take on anything new until your relationship has fully recovered. If you have just finished an emotionally draining task and have not yet recovered (either personally or maritally), to take on a new one is very risky.

"My family will always be there. Mrs. Brown's crisis is now" is a thought many a counselor or pastor has had.

Pastor Steve had agreed to attend his daughter's volleyball game at 4:00 P.M. He hadn't written it in his book—but Friday afternoons were usually light. Surely nothing could interfere.

In mid-afternoon on Friday, his secretary called him on the intercom: "It's Mrs. Brown on the phone. She really sounds upset." Mrs. Brown had found marijuana under her son's bed and she just had to speak with the pastor. Pastor Steve agreed to see her even though it meant he would miss his daughter's game. He reasoned he could go to the next game. Besides, Mrs. Brown needed him and his daughter would understand.

This is dangerous thinking. The same principle applies here as in the previous section. If Pastor Steve had attended all his daughter's games, then it is all right for him to see Mrs. Brown, and his daughter would understand. If, on the other hand, time with his daughter had been postponed again and again because of various "crises," then Dad may have a worth-through-works problem.

When Jesus said the poor will always be with us, he was telling us to get our relational priorities straight. Helping others is not bad. However, the reasonable needs of our spouses and then our children come before the needs of others.

PLAY AS A MAJOR PREVENTIVE TECHNIQUE

What else can we do? In the chapter on communications we presented the Transactional Analysis model of personality, which states that a personality is composed of the Parent, the Adult, and the Child. The characteristics of the Parent are to obey the shoulds, the oughts, and the musts of life, to know what is right and what is wrong. Another parental trait is to be nurturing and supportive, to be compassionate when others are in need, and to be willing to help. The Adult is the part of us that figures things out, makes decisions, analyzes, and evaluates while the Child in us has feelings and desires, is creative and intuitive and can be spontaneous and can play and have fun.

People helpers, pastors, nurses, teachers, and counselors have a well-developed nurturing Parent. It is their desire to nurture and to have compassion. Accountants and scientists have a well-developed Adult. Most professions draw on either the Adult or the Parent in the personality. The question here is, how strong is our Child?

An analysis (using your Adult) is useful. It would be good to involve your spouse since he or she can help you look more objectively at your Child, and you can help your partner look at his or her Child. A healthy marriage requires that both of you have a strong Child component. Play is important! Some of these questions may be useful. Can you play? Is it easy for you to have fun? If the answer is no, then you have an imbalance and it is desirable to develop the Child side of you. If the answer is yes, then look at what is fun or play for you. If play or fun is "change-of-pace work" like remodeling a basement or landscaping a yard, it is not play. It might be satisfying or enjoyable, but it is still work.

If fun is doing a project, making jam, restoring an old car, quilting, or raising bees, it is really coming more from your Adult or Parent than your Child. If fun is playing golf, running, biking, or learning Greek, you are very likely focused on learning or improving yourself more than on just playing. This is not to say these things are bad. All healthy people do a lot of these kinds of things as part of their recreation. Some fun, however, should yield absolutely no payoff, no product, no improved skill, no helped person, just pure pleasure. A leisurely walk on the beach, playing catch with the kids (just because it is fun), reading a spy novel, or taking off your shoes and walking through the grass are pleasures with no product except enjoyment.

Marital fun can be looking for wild flowers or bird watching (as long as no one keeps score), spending an hour showering together and giving each other back rubs, watching an old Laurel and Hardy movie together, or buying a bag of assorted-flavor jelly beans and trying to guess the flavors while blindfolded.

Summary

The primary theme of this chapter has been to create awareness of the need for regular maintenance of the marriage and to faithfully follow a plan to keep the marriage in good condition. A special caution is given concerning putting the needs of others before a spouse's and/or family's need.

A key element in preventing marital difficulties is to be able to have fun, both as individuals and as a couple. Much of the fun will probably yield a product or improve a skill, but some fun should be for pleasure alone.

A note of encouragement is given to you, the counselor, not to neglect your own personal and marital growth and development.

CHAPTER FOURTEEN

"TO EVERYTHING THERE IS A SEASON"

STAGE-RELATED ISSUES IN MARRIAGE COUNSELING

> Marriage, like life, is on the move, advancing from one stable period to another. Because of this, marital passages of one kind or another are inevitable. . . . Passages are truly challenges. Each one gives us the opportunity to deepen our love as we help each other along the course of our marriage.[1]

It is generally understood that all marriages pass through stages or seasons. Information about these stages can help us understand and move through "predictable" stress more productively. Change is predictable even in the early years of marriage, and as couples experience these changes, they may feel "out of sync." They may think the marriage was a mistake, when in fact they are simply adjusting to a predictable change.

It is our intent to briefly present examples of these predictable problems that couples face. Selected major areas of concern are: roles and careers, parents and parenting, family and friends, illness, change, and remarriage. This is by no means a complete study. We believe it can be useful for the counselor to understand the stages and their potential problems. For additional information, we refer the reader to H. Norman Wright's well-referenced book, *Seasons of a Marriage.*[2]

The communication and conflict-resolution skills presented earlier help clients form a cooperative attitude, which is essential for getting through stressful times. Often, the counselor will make a simple, practical suggestion that will reduce pressure for the couple. Often, we hear a couple say, "That sounded so simple but it was so useful. I don't know why I never thought of it."

For the purpose of this book we will refer to the stages of marriage as the early years, the middle years, and the later years.

ROLES

The roles that are played in a marriage come from two major sources: the tasks that need to be done and the beliefs of each marriage partner about who is to do what. The kind of work around the home that needs to be done changes as situations and circumstances change. *Who* should do the work is a more permanent feature that usually comes, at least in the early years, from one's family of origin.

The Early Years. We see two closely related issues for the couple in the early years, both of which deal with the individual's personal programming. One issue is gender-related programming (man's job versus woman's job) and the other is the issue of fairness.

Hank and Robbin were both raised on farms and in families where women did the indoor work and men did the outdoor work. Both were comfortable with the traditional sex roles. On the farm there was no problem with fairness; both genders had much to do. But unlike their families, Hank and Robbin lived in

173

a condo. And, unlike Robbin's mother, Robbin worked full time, outside the home.

It seemed natural for Robbin to do all the meal preparation and housekeeping. However, since little outside work existed, except an occasional oil change, it was unfair for the work to be divided along the traditional familial lines. In this example, gender-related programming was the strongest influence. If their way of doing things were to continue, Robbin would probably begin to feel resentment because the workload was not fair.

The counselor's primary task was to help the couple develop respect for each other.

The first step was to define the work needing to be done. The next step was to divide the tasks fairly.

We like to assign home and family chores by considering the time available to each of the partners, as well as individual gifts or talents, and individual preferences. If Hank and Robbin both worked forty hours a week, their available time should be the same. So, the chores should be equally divided, based on the amount of time necessary to complete the chores. Who would do what would then be determined by gifts and preferences.

In another couple, a husband may work full time while the wife works at home, raising three young children. She has more tasks than she can complete during the time her husband is away. The remaining tasks should be divided. A couple with both people working full time and the wife attending school three nights a week might decide that the husband does all of the chores.

In determining roles the key issue is fairness, rather than what is man's work or woman's work. Couples who have problems with this concept might profit from reading Proverbs 31:10–31, the passage on the virtuous woman. Yes, she did do the things we traditionally think of as woman's work, but she also did the things we think of as men's work.

The Middle Years. The principles for roles in this period are the same as for the "early years"; however, the tasks are different. Children need less direct care and supervision in a couple's "middle years." Eventually, children leave home; women may return to the work place. If the couple has been negotiating the division of labor all along, there will be little difficulty now.

The Later Years. The most stressful factor in the "later years" is the loss of identity related to roles. If a man's identity has been totally related to work and he has assumed no responsibility or connection with roles at home, retirement may be very difficult. If he has defined himself by having roles in a variety of settings, then the loss of the work role is less significant.

The second factor has to do with loss of physical functioning. If we get feelings of personal worth from what we do, our self-esteem sinks if we can no longer do these things. As counselors, we encourage people to broaden their activities and participate in more roles so a future decline in functioning will have less impact. We also encourage people to shift their derivation of self-worth from what they *do* to *who they are*—"a child of the king."

FAMILY AND FRIENDS

We often show couples the model in Figure 14.1 to illustrate the element of balance and bring relationships into perspective.

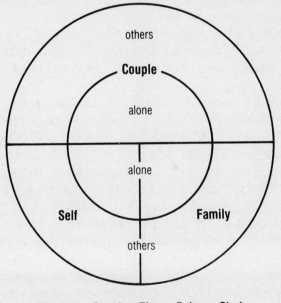

Fig. 14.1 People—Time—Balance Circle

The pie is divided into three parts: Self, Family, and Couple. About twice as much time is suggested for the Couple as for Self or Family. A second division is Others and Alone. Self-Other time is for the person and his or her friends to be together. Self-Alone time is just that. Family-Other time is for group family activities with one's family and other families. Family-Alone is time with just the family. Couple-Others is time doing things with other couples and Couple-Alone time is just that. The diagram is not to be interpreted rigidly; however, the general principles are important. More time should be given to the Couple than to Self or Family. Some Alone time is necessary as well as time with Others. If any of these are strongly under-or-over-represented for an extended period of time, difficulties may arise.

The Early Years. Different couples encounter different problems. Some are too closely tied to his or her family. Some want to spend all their time alone, as a couple. Others are so involved with friends, the couple gets no time alone.

The earliest part of the "early years" is the time to establish precedents, particularly with family. The young couple needs to have some distance between themselves and the family. We use the term *family* for the early part of this period meaning the parents of the bride and groom. When children come, the Family-Alone means husband, wife, and children. Family-Other includes grandparents, aunts, uncles, etc., and other nonrelated families.

The Middle Years. A couple can become more and more child- and family-centered, celebrating all the birthdays, holidays, Father's Day, Mother's Day, and anniversaries with the family. Couple-time and Self-time may be reduced to dangerous levels. The best way to prevent this is through careful planning. Couples can sit down with a calendar and look ahead three or four months to note events like birthdays. They then can decide how to spend time. (The Friesen family often decides to celebrate several family events at one occasion. We celebrate three birthdays that fall in March together. In our family there are many family reunions. Sometimes we will choose to not attend one of these in order to create time for a higher priority, Couple or Self.)

The Later Years. One of the most frequent complaints is heard from wives who feel they are the only source of social interaction for their retired husbands. Husbands often have not developed the Self-Alone time (hobbies, reading, gardening) or the Self-Other. They often have no friends other than their wives. The best solution to this problem is prevention. As soon as possible, husbands should develop hobbies and make friends other than the spouse and family.

FINANCES

The Early Years. In the early years of marriage, many couples desire to live better than their income will allow. A not uncommon solution, particularly if the young couple is still in school, is for one or both sets of parents to give financial help. This continues the dependence of the children and perpetuates the authority of the parents. Couples must try to achieve realistic expectations. If the parents choose to help out financially, a balance must be achieved between financial dependence and independence in a timely manner.

Robert and Joanne were a young couple with three small children. In their family, Robert handled the finances and determined the food budget. Joanne purchased the food and provided healthy meals. Joanne felt that shopping for food on the budgeted amount of money was next to impossible. Robert agreed to do the shopping for a week and soon realized he must increase the food budget. This was a simple solution, which involved one person stepping into another's shoes for a short time.

The Middle Years. Defining and setting appropriate limits for spending may be an important issue at this time. Also during these middle years, some couples need to set limits to avoid using available income to overindulge the children.

A common counseling problem will be concerned with how the couple manages their money. For example, partners may disagree on the use of credit cards, the timely payment of bills, or one may have a tendency to write checks on insufficient funds. If both partners are committed to change, the counselor usually can help them develop a plan and get started.

Loretta and Tim realized they used credit cards too much. As a first step, they returned new unused goods. Secondly, they decided on one card to be used for emergencies, and closed out several other accounts. They also worked out a budget, building in money for recreation as well as an amount for each to spend as he or she pleased. Recognizing that they tended to spend all available money, they decided to have part of their income automatically deposited into a savings plan.

A more difficult situation occurs with Marla and Frank. Frank refused to share information about how bills were paid and about their financial situation. Marla didn't know when a collection person might call or if the water would be turned off or whether enough money was in the account for her to write a check, without first asking Frank. Neither did she know what resources were being set aside for retirement.

Frank refused to enter counseling so Marla needed to make some changes on her own. She began to handle her paycheck herself, paying the expenses that her check covered. She kept careful records and showed them to her husband and, chose to improve her job skills in order to be able to generate more income. She learned about finances, income tax, and retirement benefits, although she had previously felt she wasn't smart enough to handle such things. She also determined that she, as a Christian wife, had the right to participate in the handling of the family finances. (Previously, she had thought a submissive wife didn't have this right if her husband so determined.) In this case, the counseling focused on what she could do to change her situation and stay in the marriage. In time, her depression lifted and she was able to move ahead with her life.

The Later Years. Predictable stress during these years seems to come from two directions. Couples may have trouble adjusting to their retirement income. Often, they are dealing with how to make it stretch to meet their needs. Another common scenario involves the new widow who has little knowledge of her financial situation or how to handle her money.

Regardless of the cause, the aging couple may need help in handling finances and may depend heavily on adult children for this assistance. Husbands and wives need to agree beforehand on the amount and nature of assistance the aging parents will be given. We have found that most daughters-in-law and sons-in-law are generous when they are included in the

178

decision-making process. On the other hand, they can be resentful when decisions are made for them.

These adult children may be entering the "later years" themselves. A difficult question and responsibility for them is how to determine if guardianship is needed. The counselor may choose to refer these cases to professionals who specialize in aging.

Sometimes it is necessary to learn how to take care of ourselves as we take care of our aging parents. Not only are we happier, but in the long run, the aging parent and the spouse are happier too.

Helen's mother was eighty-one years old. She liked to go to the bank and handle her own investments. Helen had to accompany her on these trips, but her mother refused any other help. By the time the ordeal was over Helen would be fighting a sick headache. Helen knew that the transactions seemed to go all right since the people at the bank knew her mother and were very patient in explaining each transaction to her. The work Helen and the counselor did together was to help her develop more patience. One of counseling's goals was to fine-tune Helen's listening skills to the point that she was giving less advice. Cognitive therapy was useful in helping her determine how she was upsetting herself. We also built in a reward (a cup of coffee, a yogurt cone) for Helen for after the banking trips. Banking day with Mom is still not Helen's first choice for a fun day, but the headaches are gone.

PARENTS AND PARENTING

The Early Years. The earliest part of the "early years" focuses on our emancipation from our parents. This is easy if our parents have prepared us for this all along. The issues discussed in the section on friends and family are pertinent here.

When children are born, a couple's focus switches to parenting. Parenting is often stressful for the couple, and not necessarily because the husband and wife hold to different long-range values for their children. We have found that most people want their children to grow up to be hard-working, honest, considerate, God-loving, and parent-loving human beings. However, we often find that one parent is likely to be more liberal, and the other to be more conservative in issues

179

that concern child-raising. One is more trusting, the other more suspicious. One is more play oriented, the other more work oriented. Neither parent is wrong; they are simply different from each other, and this difference creates tension. The task for the couple is to learn how to handle these differences.

The parenting resources we especially recommend are: *Parent Survival Training, Try Being a Teenager, Parenthood Without Hassle (Well Almost)*, and *Parenting Isn't for Cowards*.[3] The important issue is that parents, behind closed doors, must negotiate a compromise or agreement on rules, exceptions to rules, and consequences for broken rules. These will be somewhat too strict for one parent and a little lenient for the other, but the united front is beneficial for all.

A united front produces stability in the family. Otherwise, the child learns that he or she can play one parent against the other. The more lenient parent (at least on the issue in question) is approached by the child first. If permission is granted, then the child does what he or she was given permission to do. The other parent often disapproves and that creates friction between the parents.

When our children were teenagers we had a policy that extraordinary requests had to be made a day before the event (if possible). This allowed us time to evaluate and discuss. Sometimes Ruby thought the request was reasonable and Dee didn't and sometimes it was the other way around. Sometimes we both initially were in agreement. When we disagreed we did so in private and presented our decision—a united front— to the child. Parents do not always need twenty-four hours to weigh the decision but some time behind closed doors is essential.

Research has shown that low self-esteem in children results from either authoritarian (Do it my way because I'm your Dad/ Mom . . . because I said so) or permissive (Do whatever you'd like) parenting. High self-esteem, on the other hand, is produced by an authoritative parent. This parent says, "These are the rules and their reasons. We expect you to follow them. The rules can be changed as conditions change. There will be exceptions from time to time. We expect, however, the exceptions to be the exception not the rule." This parent is in charge, but is flexible. There is room for the child to take an active and appropriate part in the decision-making process.

Another parenting issue of the early years concerns the time required to care for babies. Spouses need care too, so at this time it is very important for the husband to be nurturing to the wife and for the wife to not neglect her husband. Later problems may be prevented if the husband is not dethroned by the arrival of the child.

The Middle Years. The primary task in our relationship with our children is letting them go. We have been teaching, disciplining, and modeling. What the children haven't learned by now, they will have to learn themselves through trial and error. Forming new in-law relationships is easier if we have released our sons or daughters.

A recent common occurrence for couples in these years (and the later years) is the "boomerang child"—the adult child who returns home. Some of these children are regrouping and are working hard to deal with getting on with their lives; others are adult children who have been rescued by their parents all their lives. Children from this group may be with Mom and Dad for a long time.

Having children return requires adjustment since the parents have come to enjoy being just the two again. Parents in this situation should do careful planning before the children move back home, by setting time limits and rules. While it is nice to be helpful to the children in their time of need, the marriage relationship is still primary and must not be compromised.

The second task of the "middle years," especially in the latter part, is to become more of a parent to our own parent. When one of your parents dies, the other is likely to be more dependent upon the grown children, both for emotional support and for practical, day-to-day decision making. The degree of dependency depends a great deal upon the personality and resources of the parent. It is also a fact that parents in these circumstances may not need help as much as we think they do. They have successfully made decisions for some time and they do not automatically need their children to help them. It is important that a balance of loving support and independence is achieved. We must not, out of love or respect or pity or guilt or manipulation, do for our aging parent what he or she is able to do. In the long run this detracts from the parent's sense of competence and self-esteem.

We know of an eighty-year-old lady who lived three blocks from a senior center. There were many activities in which she could have participated; the center would have picked her up and brought her home. But she refused to have anything to do with the program. Instead, by using guilt, she manipulated her unmarried daughter to take her on errands and provide her with social contacts. More and more the daughter resented her mother and her demands.

In this situation the problem was caused as much by the daughter's response as it was by the mother's demands. The daughter could have said: "Mom, if you go to the senior center twice a week and use their bus service to go grocery shopping, I'll take you to have your hair done and then take you to lunch on Saturdays. If you don't, I won't!" The mother would have initially complained and used every argument she could marshal to change her daughter's mind; but we find that if the adult children hold their ground, their aging parents usually come around.

The Later Years. These are a continuation of the "middle years" and involve less effort in the parenting of our children, and greater parenting of our parents. As our parents die, and as we age, we need to make new friends, seek new activities, and not depend on our children to do for us what we can do for ourselves.

What is the role of the grandparents? We believe that balance must be a priority here. Determining what is a healthy involvement in and contribution to the lives of the grandchildren must be a joint project. Once again, spouses must be sure to maintain time for each other.

ILLNESS

Illness may bring the most traumatic changes to a marriage. Particularly in the "early years," we expect our spouses and our children to be healthy. But illness may strike and in some cases the problem may never go away or is never solved. In many families, every role is affected. The wife may now have to be the

bread winner, or the parents may have to parent a multihandi-
capped child when she is eighteen years old. The responsibilities can be enormous. Healing and adjusting include grieving
for what might have been. Besides grieving, the parents must
each recommit themselves to love the other, and to love the
child who is ill. Couples need to be deeply committed to
the marriage in order to make things work.

The couple should be advised to look at the options available.
In many situations the couple must face the question of whether
the marriage can stand the strain and stress. (Does the child lose
twice if the parents divorce? Probably yes.) What are workable
options in order for the marriage to stay intact? The answers
will be different for different couples. Some marriages are not
strong enough, even with help.

Illness at any stage of life produces stress. Acute illness, such
as an accident or surgery, however, usually produces short-term
stress. Everything is disrupted for a time but it eventually
passes. Even an acute illness that results in a quick death is often
easier to handle than a severely disabling chronic illness.

It is the chronic illness that places the most stress on the
marriage and the individuals. If a chronic illness involves a child
or an aging parent living with a couple, some safeguards for the
marriage need to be in place. Caring for the ill person does take
time and that time has to come from somewhere. Some individual, couple, and family time will need to be sacrificed. However, some individual, couple, and family time needs to be held
sacred.

Husband and wife need to share in the care of the ill person.
This way, no one person is sacrificing all of his or her personal
time. Bringing someone in to care for the person allows the
couple to have time away and time alone. As with the eighty-
year-old lady who would not participate in the senior center
program, the person who is ill may protest. The protest can be
understood but not heeded. Even though we do have an obligation to our dependent family members, the primary long-term
obligation is to our spouses. Granted, finding someone to care
for one's ill parents or children is difficult. There are home
nursing programs, if the person needs that level of care. There is
a new idea called "respite care" for the severely and chronically

ill. In this type of care a trained professional comes in for a few hours to relieve the family. Checking with a local hospital, social service agency, or nursing association may identify resources in your area.

As an eventuality with chronically ill parents who are aged, a nursing home may become the best option. Many adult children reach the point where they no longer can care for a parent or a spouse even with outside help. It is a difficult but necessary decision to place the person in a facility where full-time care is available.

REMARRIAGE

Many divorced and widowed people will remarry. While a man and woman in remarrying must deal with many of the same issues as does the couple entering its first marriage, some issues are unique to remarriage. We encourage you to read one of the many books available on remarriage. A classic is *Stepfamilies*, by John and Emily Visher.[4]

The Early Years. If death or divorce has terminated a marriage before children are born, the person has much in common with partners in a first marriage. Ties to the previous in-laws as well as to the ex-spouse will be weaker. However, a common problem in this situation is known as the "ghost" issue. The new couple must deal with the ghost of the former spouse. Many couples find that moving into living quarters that are new to both spouses is helpful. The pastor should also be aware of the potential for a "rebound" remarriage; he or she can be very supportive of the person and the developing relationship while, at the same time, encouraging a lengthy courtship. A year-long courtship and engagement period is far less likely to lead to a hasty marriage than one that is but two months long.

If there are young children involved, the situation becomes more complicated. A satisfactory or at least predictable custody and visitation arrangement should be worked out. The needs of the children to keep a relationship with three sets of grandparents should be considered. One resource book on custody that we have found helpful is *Mom's House, Dad's House.*[5]

In a "blended family" where both spouses bring in children from previous marriages, the situation becomes even more complicated.

Blended families usually have divided loyalties because children as a rule maintain a relationship with and some positive feeling for the absent parent. Also, the children may have trouble adjusting to each other and may not even get along well with their new step-brother or sister. . . . It is important that you never play favorites, even though one of you is the natural parent of each child. Together you must work as a team and deal consistently, honestly, and directly with each of them.[6]

When counseling parents in blended families with young children, you will find the united-front attitude discussed in the parenting section helpful.

The united front is even more important with blended families. It is normal for a child to go to his or her biological parent for permission. When agreements are made between the child and the parent without consulting the stepparent, the stepparent feels excluded (jealous). This produces negative feelings both toward the spouse and the stepchild. It is fine, at least at first in the new remarriage, for the child to approach his or her natural parent with requests. It is the natural parent's responsibility then to discuss the request with the stepparent before a final decision is made. Of course, we are talking about more important requests here, not trivial ones. The more trivial issues should be decided on the spot by whichever parent is asked.

When the remarriage takes place in the latter part of the "early years" or the early part of the "middle years," and the children are adolescents, the problems become compounded. Several years ago during a discussion on remarriage involving teenagers, Harold Ivan Smith commented (perhaps tongue in cheek) that people ought to wait to remarry until the teenage children have left home. One remarriage we worked with consisted of the wife and her two teenage daughters and the new husband. There was so much stress that the new husband moved into his own apartment. The marriage continued, but the man and woman chose not to live under the same roof until the girls were emancipated.

With teens, especially older teens, it is usually better for the natural parent to do the major disciplining. Both parents can agree on rules and consequences, but the child's own Mom or Dad should implement the consequences for breaking the rules.

Affirming the marital bond is especially important in a remarriage with a blended family. Of course, the natural parent must spend significant time with his or her own children as well as some time with his or her spouse's children. As important as the children are, however, the primary allocation of time and energy needs to be with the new spouse. As traumatic as it was for the children to have gone through divorce, the last thing they need is another divorce. Children do not always cooperate in the endeavor since they live more in the present than in the future. They would rather spend time with Mom and Dad than have the folks go off together.

The Middle Years. If the children have left the nest, troublesome issues in these years may be at a low level.

The Later Years. One of the biggest issues for later years occurs when a partner comes into a remarriage with wealth. More often than not, in the later years a death rather than divorce has terminated the previous marriage. Children who are now in their forties to sixties expected Mom or Dad to live to a ripe old age (and that *they* would inherit what the parents didn't use). The inheritance may be jeopardized when Mom or Dad wants to remarry.

Prenuptial agreements, issues of inheritance in particular, and finances in general need to be fully and openly worked through before remarriage. We encourage older single parents to make decisions about any inheritance known to the children before a potential spouse enters the scene.

A less frequent but important problem occurs with the adult child who views Mom or Dad's remarriage as disloyalty to the deceased. Counseling for the adult child would be helpful in this case.

Summary

In this chapter we have shared a concept that has two important points. First, many things that happen to people in life are predictable and are normal aspects of that stage of life. Second, we can lessen the impact of these events by preparing for them. If we prepare, the transition from one life stage or event to another can be made without undo stress. Without preparation, a transition may become a crisis.

The marital life stages are defined as "early years," "middle years," and "later years." The potential problems arise with roles, friends and family, parents and parenting, illness, change, and remarriage.

This chapter was not meant to provide an exhaustive list of marital issues across all of the marital life stages; instead we dealt with issues commonly encountered in our counseling experience. Our bigger goal is to present the concept of anticipating and preparing for the changes related to stages in living.

CHAPTER FIFTEEN

SPOUSE ABUSE

Spouse abuse is being addressed in this separate chapter because we do not wish to minimize the trauma and difficulty such a situation causes for couples. We also wish to emphasize the need for you, the counselor, to understand the dynamics of spouse abuse. It is not the intent of this chapter to give you all the tools for working with spouse abuse. We do, however, wish to point you in a helpful direction since you will, over the course of time, encounter problems related to abuse.

TYPES OF VIOLENCE

Neidig and Friedman, the authors of *Spouse Abuse: A Treatment Program for Couples,* describe two types of violence or abuse: instrumental and expressive. They make an important distinction:

> Instrumental violence is the deliberate use of violence as an instrument or tool for social influence. It is almost always violence inflicted by men on women and can be accurately referred to as "wife battering." It is employed to punish or to control the behavior of the spouse.[1]

In this situation the degree or level of provocation is low and violence escalates rapidly. Later, remorse may be expressed, but this is more of a manipulative move. The appropriate intervention may be separation, arranging for protective shelter, and possible legal sanction.

This is not to say that this type of violence can never be treated. It does say you are dealing with a different situation from that of expressive violence.

> Expressive violence is considered to be primarily an expression or function of a high level of emotional arousal. It typically occurs in the context of gradually escalating conflict between husband and wife.

This violence usually involves the participation of each spouse. There is the tension-building phase, followed by the out-of-control abusive phase, ending in the genuine remorse phase.

Motivation for change is usually higher for the expressive violent couple and is highest just following an abusive episode. It is important that treatment be attempted at this time. There is evidence that once the first episode has occurred it becomes easier for the next one to happen, and the couple could eventually move into the "instrumental" category.

Grant Martin, in *Counseling for Family Violence and Abuse*,[2] describes the following personality characteristics of men who batter and women who are battered. The abuser has an *inability to manage anger*. Healthy conflict-management skills were not modeled in the family of origin. *Inexpressiveness* contributes to the anger problem. Since the abuser also *lacks assertiveness*, he doesn't clearly express his desires to his spouse. And yet, he erupts in anger when she doesn't do what he wants. The abusing man usually has *low self-esteem*. This contributes to an *emotional dependence* on his wife. He fears he will lose his wife and continually seeks her reassurance. Since he fears losing her, jealousy is a common problem. Unfortunately, fear leads to jealousy and jealousy leads to anger. His fear generates a need to control his spouse. In part, this is achieved by a *rigid and domineering application of traditional sex attitudes.*

The last personality characteristic of the abuser is *alcohol and drug dependency*, since it is present in two-thirds of the abuse situations. Like their male counterparts, the battered women have *low self-esteem* and *emotional dependency*. Unlike the men, the women also have *economic dependency*. Because the husband fears his wife will leave him, he isolates her from others. Along with *isolation*, two other factors contribute to her remaining in an abusive situation—*unrealistic hope* and *a strong traditional view of marriage.*

Characteristics of spouse abusers are similar to those of the alcoholic. Both use denial and blaming, and both promise to stop.

The abusing spouse does not usually deny that the partner was hurt during an argument. Rather, the denial is in the form of minimizing the severity of the abusive interaction. "She is just making a big deal out of nothing," the man might say. "I didn't hit her; I just pulled her off the bed. She cut her head because she slipped on the throw rug and fell against the dresser. She is making me out to be a monster and I resent it." The truth of this interaction is that he yanked his wife off the bed and threw her against the dresser. If he tells this story over and over, he begins to believe his version of the incident. Since it all happened so fast, and he seems so sure of his position, his wife may come to believe his version as well.

Blaming the partner frequently accompanies minimizing the abuse. When blaming occurs, the reason for the abuse is shifted to the abused partner. "All I wanted to do was go for a drive to cool off. She wouldn't give me my car keys so I had to take them away from her. If she hadn't have stood so close to the car, I wouldn't have driven over her foot." This kind of rationalization is typical of the blamer.

When promises are made to stop the abuse, the abuser is admitting that he or she has gotten out of control. However, the belief that control can be gained by trying harder next time is usually erroneous. The next time emotional control is lost, loss of physical control is likely to follow. Promising to change is a type of self-denial. *I can change on my own. Therefore, the problem is not that bad.* If promises have already been made and broken, it is a sure sign to the marriage counselor that expert help with this couple is required.

The abusing couple usually seeks treatment at the insistence of the abused partner. The abuser, with all his psychological defense mechanisms, is not likely to pursue help on his own. The abusing husband may use Ephesians 5:22–23 to convince his wife that she has to obey him.

Wives, submit to your husbands as to the Lord. For the husband is the head of the wife as Christ is the head of the church, his body, of which he is the Savior.

Marie Fortune, in her book, *Keeping the Faith: Questions and Answers for the Abused Woman,* explains the biblical concept presented in this passage:

This means that there are times in a Christian marriage when a wife should give way to her husband and recognize his interests as well as her own. But the husband's headship suggested here does not mean a role of unquestioned authority to which you are to be blindly obedient. What is described here is a model based on Christ's relationship to the church: Jesus was the servant of all who followed him and he gave himself up for them. Never did he order people around, threaten, hit, or frighten them.

Almost all the rest of this passage from Ephesians spells out the instructions to the husband in his treatment of the wife: he is to be to her as Christ was to the church. This means he is to serve her needs and be willing to sacrifice himself for her if need be. This is what Jesus did for the church. He is to love his wife as himself, to nourish and cherish her. Another passage is even more specific:

> Husbands, love your wives and do not be harsh with them.
> (Col. 3:19)

Clearly, the emphasis Scripture places on instructing husbands to care for and respect their wives just as Christ did the church leaves no room for excusing a husband's violent and abusive behavior toward his wife. Neither does your responsibility to accommodate to him and respect him mean that Jesus expects you to stay and tolerate his abuse. If he is not fulfilling his responsibility as a husband to you—that is, treating you with respect—you are not obligated to be a doormat for him. Your obligation is to provide for your safety and your children's safety.[3]

With this correct view of headship and submission, the Christian wife will be more sure of her right to insist on treatment for the abuse or reserve the right to leave the relationship if treatment is refused.

Neither the alcoholic or spouse abuser respond well to self-treatment. Referring abusive couples to someone trained in this area is the preferred action. In addition, spouse-abuse support groups designed along the lines of Alcoholics Anonymous can be helpful.

TREATMENT

Treatment involves the development of security measures—contracts to stop and to use time-out and developing skills for control of anger, stress management, communication, and conflict containment.

Working with abusive couples requires first that you become aware of the abuse. Couples tend to minimize abuse. Even if you ask them to describe how conflict resolution occurs, you may not discover the abuse at first. You may gain some clues through your initial interview form if you ask the right questions.

James Trotzer states that he almost always invites the children in for one session when he is doing marriage counseling, to help him understand what it is like to live in the house of this husband and wife.[4] You may discover abuse in this information. Being sensitive to the possibility of abuse is perhaps your greatest tool.

Our experience in working with abusive couples has shown

that at first it is important to proceed step by step through the development of the abusive process, how the couple will act it out, and what they will do to calm down during the times-out. Couples will need for you to be specific about such techniques as how to use a mental time-out in the car or at other times when they can't separate.

Understanding the cycle of abuse is important. Both partners often contribute to the tension-building phase, which comes first. This is followed by the out-of-control or abusive phase, which is followed by the remorse or regret phase. The individuals need to learn how to identify tension building, as displayed in bodily or verbal cues. They need to learn to identify triggers of tension that they can recognize and techniques they can use in controlling the situation at the tension-building level. Developing techniques for anger control is also vital.

The Decision to Stay or to Leave

The healing of the marriage is primary with the abused spouse. But that healing does not just mean that the couple is still together. It means the individual is a productive, emotionally healthy human being as well. If an individual is being physically or emotionally destroyed to keep the marriage together, something is wrong.

The abused spouse is often confused. "Have I done enough?" "Shouldn't I try one more time?" "Shouldn't I do everything possible to keep the marriage?" These questions are repeatedly asked. In situations such as these we sometimes use this analogy to help a person gain perspective.

Let's pretend you are an airplane pilot. One of the safety precautions you take is to keep a parachute with you. You are flying at seven thousand feet when the engine cuts out. You know that you can safely deploy the parachute at two thousand feet and live. That means you have some five thousand feet to try to work things out and get the plane flying again. You may try all you know to start the engine. If the engine starts, wonderful. You have saved the airplane. But if repeated efforts fail, and you have reached two thousand feet, it is time to jump.

You can help the counselee assess whether there is enough emotional and physical stamina remaining, and if there is enough hope of a positive outcome to warrant continuing in the marriage. There are times when this analogy helps a counselee realize that if he or she does not jump now, both the pilot (he or she) and the plane (the marriage) will be lost. By jumping, at least the pilot will be saved.

While abuse may not be an issue for the majority of the couples, it happens frequently enough within the church that every pastoral counselor will find it advantageous to understand the abuse cycle and treatment methods.

CHAPTER SIXTEEN

SEPARATION AND DIVORCE

A middle-aged man approached us at a church leaders' workshop we were presenting. "Did the Beaverton Family Counseling Center used to be located on Canyon Road?" he asked. "Yes," was our reply, "we were there until about eight years ago." His face became grim. "You were the outfit," he said, "that got me my divorce."

Unfortunately, divorce still occurs, even after hours are spent in counseling with a pastor or Christian counselor. Harvey Ruben, M.D., Chair of the Public Affairs Commission of the American Psychiatric Association, says in his book, *Supermarriage*, that about 50 percent of the couples who come for counseling concerning marital issues either eventually divorce or continue to live in unhappy marriages.[1]

We believe the percentage of troubled Christian couples who divorce after seeking Christian counseling is lower than Ruben's figures, but divorce certainly does occur. Part of our reason for sharing this is to assert that the counselor cannot, and should not, feel responsible for the choices the counselees make. We all try to do a good job, share the appropriate tools, and inspire hope, but, in the final analysis, it is our clients who make the choices for their marriages.

With reference to the man in the opening paragraph, we did not cause or promote divorce for him or his wife. Neither, however, were we able to prevent it.

Is Separation Ever Recommended?

Receiving marriage counseling is like having minor surgery in the physician's office. The treatment frequently corrects the problem, but in many cases the situation is much more serious; major surgery is needed. In marriage counseling, separation is major surgery and is just as risky. We recommend separation only if the "patient" is at greater risk without it.

There are two types of separation. One is temporary and occurs in the hope of the ultimate restoration of the relationship. We recommend this when the tension is so high in the marriage that physical abuse is likely. We believe that if we can help the couple dilute the intensity of the hostility in the relationship, there might be hope for the marriage.

An emotionally or physically abusive relationship lowers both the self-respect of the abused and of the abusing partner. Respect for each other is lowered as well. Separation is recommended while some respect is still left. We have learned that when all respect is gone, the chance for healing the marriage is very slight.

When divorce is seriously threatened by one or both of the partners, an assessment needs to be made as to whether keeping the couple together under the present circumstances will help them remain together in the future. Remember the dilemma. If you don't operate, the patient may die; if you do, the patient may die.

Unfortunately, some Christian counselors mistakenly put their values ahead of the client's welfare. These counselors are so opposed to separation and divorce that they keep the couple together even though the relationship is deteriorating. When this marriage dissolves, the counselor can say, "I did everything I could to keep them together."

We, on the other hand, are more concerned about the ultimate outcome than we are the purity of the technique. One reason for this is that we don't believe in magic. Insisting that people stay together is not going to make it happen. Of course, we don't go to the other extreme either. We don't insist, even in a bad situation, that the couple separate. Instead, what we do is help them look at the options. What is likely to happen if you separate for a while? What is likely to happen if you stay together? The final decision is theirs.

A second kind of separation is really a trial divorce. A person may make up his or her mind to get out of the marriage but he or she doesn't know: (a) Will the financial strain be too much? (b) Will the emotional strain be too much? (c) How will it affect the children? "So, I will separate for a while and look at the impact," they say. "If things look workable and it feels okay, I'll file for divorce." These are typical thoughts of the person considering the second type of separation. That person wants a divorce but is hedging the bet through a trial separation. We do not support this kind of separation, because of its implicit dishonesty. The other partner enters into the separation in good faith, believing restoration of the marriage to be the goal. We explain both types of separation and point out the unfairness and dishonesty of the trial-divorce separation. If a separation occurs, a greater commitment to the eventual restoration of the marriage is often the result of this discussion.

IS DIVORCE EVER RECOMMENDED?

Do we ever tell people to get a divorce? The answer is no, never. This is too important an issue. We do not have to live with the consequences of the choice; therefore, we will never decide for a person.

Sometimes we help the client look at alternatives. What is likely to happen if they remain in the marriage? What is likely to happen if they allow the spouse to return home? What is likely to happen if they: (a) leave for a temporary separation, (b) file for legal separation, or (c) file for divorce? We want the individual who is considering divorce to explore the emotional, relational, spiritual, and financial impacts on both the spouse and the children. We also want them to explore the history of the marriage relationship. What worked? What didn't? Why didn't it work?

Do we ever give a negative evaluation or prediction for remaining in the marriage? At times we do. The psychological evidence for certain types of personality disorders is convincing. The likelihood of positive change, for the antisocial personality, the borderline personality, or the chronic chemically dependent personality, is not good, unless there is very high motivation. The highly histrionic or narcissistic or paranoid personality may be less destructive to a marriage, but is not likely to change either. Does this mean a person married to this kind of personality should divorce? That is not what we are saying. It means that if a person is married to one of these pathological personality types, he or she had better decide to stay in the marriage for some reason other than the belief the spouse will change. Change with these personality types is unlikely.

We know that people can change. We know that genuine miracles happen. We also know that some so-called miracles are short-lived and that, before long, the transformed person has returned to his or her former state.

We ask you to remember the airplane analogy. If the airplane's engine quits at seven thousand feet and the altimeter now reads four thousand feet, our client still has two thousand feet to go before he or she must bail out. We encourage some of our clients to consider giving the marriage another chance if the spouse seems to sincerely want to change. We don't encourage another chance if the act of contrition on the part of the spouse appears manipulative or if the physical and emotional resources of our client are at rock bottom. Even then, all we can do is point out clearly the options, along with the likely outcomes. The final choice must be the client's.

Earlier in this section we used some personality labels. We did not elaborate on these because diagnosing these accurately is usually beyond the training of a pastoral counselor. Such definitive diagnosis is best done by a clinical psychologist or a psychiatrist.

The examination of issues concerning whether or not to divorce is a task the counselee should carry out with a counselor. The decision is too important for the troubled spouse to make alone. Reading, however, can be a helpful addition to counseling. You may want to read several divorce-related books by Christian authors, and then suggest the ones you are comfortable with. Several useful books are *But I Didn't Want a Divorce* by Andre Bustanoby, *Divorce and Remarriage in the Church* by Stanley A. Ellisen, and *The Divorce Decision* by Gary Richmond.[2]

IF DIVORCE OCCURS

If a couple divorces, the counseling is not usually over. The divorced individuals frequently need help adjusting to life as single persons. Even a dysfunctional marriage has an established routine. New ways of managing the everyday tasks and responsibilities must be developed. Divorced people often do not fit in their social group as they once did. New networks of friends must be formed. Loneliness is a common problem for the newly divorced. The church needs to be instrumental in helping the divorced find a place and a purpose in life. Many churches have established divorce-support groups which have helped those who are alone. If a support group is not available, we recommend certain books that may be helpful in the adjustment process.[3]

Separation and divorce are some unpleasant realities. Sometimes they result when immature people seek to avoid responsibility and pursue their own pleasure and leave spouse and children to pay the consequences. Sometimes separation or divorce is a carefully reasoned attempt to bring closure to a destructive, painful relationship. The counselor's task is not to make the decision for the individual but to help him or her see clearly the likely outcomes of potential choices.

CHAPTER SEVENTEEN

TERMINATION OF COUNSELING

Often a counselor does not have the opportunity of going through the process of termination. It's our opinion that pastoral counselors may experience the termination process more than those of us in private practice—perhaps because the clients are paying to see the private counselor and may feel that if things are improving, they will no longer come in for counseling. Sometimes our former clients, returning several years later to work on another issue, tell us, "It was so helpful before. I remember how important it was to discover. . . ." At the same time, we remember that we were making good progress when all of a sudden there was no closure; the next appointment was just canceled. A follow-up phone call revealed that things were going well, and that the couple felt they would take a break from counseling.

Of course, the counselor prefers to have opportunity to discuss with the couple the progress being made toward goals that were established in the beginning of their counseling. Counselor and client mutually agree on how to handle termination. This is fun for those of us who have a need for closure.

Termination is indicated when (a) the couple has worked through the issue, or developed skills to be able to handle the issue that brought them to counseling, or (b) the issue may not be totally worked through but the counseling has hit a plateau; time is needed for the couple to assimilate the progress made. Only later will the couple be able to progress further.

In this latter case, in particular, the counselor will benefit from a periodic review of original counseling goals in order to assess progress. Sometimes it works to be patient. Other times, the most productive step is to discuss with the couple the plateau and the need for passage of time.

REVIEW AND REINFORCE

When we have the opportunity to work toward termination we like to accomplish several things. One is to review and reinforce with the couple what has happened during counseling. This is similar to going over a corrected exam. One can clarify some points, learn others, and reinforce what is already known. An important part of this review is that the couple will recognize how their work has made things change.

When Harold and Ann entered counseling, Harold's goal was to figure out how to divorce in a constructive manner (Harold's goal was accepted as a starting point). He respected Ann and possibly still loved her. Ann's goal was to learn about what went wrong, make changes, and save the marriage. She loved and respected Harold and valued an intact family for the children. This couple was able to work their way through a separation during which they each did some personal work. They were able to discover where things went wrong for them and developed different attitudes regarding marriage and tools for handling conflict. As a result of the progress they made, Harold decided to commit himself to the marriage.

During termination we discussed what they saw as important growth. Ann was able to verbalize her awareness of the rigid, judgmental, critical thinking which she saw was her tendency. She was able to describe the usefulness of the belief that allowed Harold the right to see things differently than she. Also, she had found that she could allow Harold to be different and still respect him.

Harold felt his major growth was in the area of learning to communicate his wants, needs, and desires. He had learned it was better to do this instead of keeping things inside until the situation was intolerable. The counselor also summarized some of her observations for the couple.

PREVENTION

A termination session allows a discussion of how to prevent regression into dysfunctional ways of relating. The counselor seeks to know: What are signs that the couple may not be dealing successfully with issues? What can they do about this?

Ted and Sue's marriage was the second for both of them. They were establishing a blended family with children at home, ranging in age from fifteen to twenty-three. One of the couple's goals for counseling was to develop a sense of working together or cooperating.

To further complicate things, Ted was a fireman and worked a two-day-on, two-day-off schedule. One of his children had a behavior problem. Sue also worked and was taking a class. When counseling was initiated, virtually all of their limited personal time was spent in dealing with various blended-family issues, or resolving conflicts.

In the termination session, we evaluated their ways of dealing with their issues. For example, they had been keeping a calendar of events and needed to review it occasionally to determine how much "alone time" they really had created. Also, they had worked on ownership of problems. "Am I trying to fix something for one of the children that really belongs to that child?" they asked. "Does the child need to choose to fix it?" "What do I need to do for me to make my world okay?" "If I recognize I'm working on the wrong problem or one that is not mine, can I refocus and perhaps accomplish something productive for me?"

The termination session provided a way to affirm the success of this change in attitude. They could both see that it prevented many of the problems they had had before counseling.

FOLLOW-UP SESSIONS

Neil Jacobson, a professor in the clinical psychology program at the University of Washington, recently stated that his clinic had implemented a recall program similar to dentist recalls. His belief is that couples will regress to a degree, and they will benefit from these check-up sessions.[1] He did not report the success rate of the recall appointments.

During termination, as mentioned earlier, we like to discuss some warning signs of regression. This does not necessarily mean the couple will need to come back for a session if that should happen. They may be able to get back on course by themselves. However, a booster shot or check-up session may be an important help in getting back on track. As a result, we try to legitimize these sessions by inviting couples to come back.

We think of termination as a process, because counseling can be very intense. For some people termination is best achieved over a period of time. It is usual to move to an every-other-week schedule, followed by an appointment a month later, and ending with an appointment three months later. Knowing we are going to gradually taper off with our sessions, the couples tell us that this continued counseling contact helps them build confidence.

Termination sessions provide an opportunity to strengthen the therapeutic process. You can use them to review and reinforce what the couple has achieved. They can also be used for preventive work. Formal termination may not be necessary for every couple. Some are able to move ahead on their own. "Booster shot" or follow-up appointments work well to remind couples of certain techniques they may have forgotten, to offset any regression, and to encourage continued work on their marriage.

CHAPTER EIGHTEEN

PREMARRIAGE COUNSELING

TWO PERSPECTIVES OF COUNSELING:
MATE SELECTION OR REMEDIATION

The skills used in premarriage counseling are no different from those used in marriage counseling. The communication techniques, problem-solving strategies, and intimacy-building approaches useful in marriage are equally useful in the premarital stage of a relationship.

Yet there is an important basic difference between marriage counseling and premarriage counseling. When we are confronted with a troubled marriage, we do everything within our power to help the couple rebuild their marriage. When we see a couple whom we think ought never to have married, our approach is one of remediation or "how can we make this poor marriage better?" At the same time we may think, "If only we could have done some premarriage counseling with them, they might have altered their expectations before they got married, or they might have decided not to marry each other at all." Before the marriage it is all right for a couple to have second thoughts. There is nothing wrong—perhaps it is even virtuous—in deciding a potential partner is not the right one.

When the principles of remediation are applied to premarriage, selection takes a back seat. The engaged or about-to-be-engaged couple hear sermons and read books on communication, resolving conflict, and building intimacy. It is easy for them to conclude that their problems can be overcome by working harder. While there is some truth to the notion that a good marriage takes work, it shouldn't take too much work. Couples must work to get over the rough spots. But when the premarriage relationship seems to be mainly rough spots, selecting a new partner may make more sense than trying to rehabilitate the present one.

PRESSURE TO MARRY

Christian young people receive powerful messages regarding marriage. Society and tradition say it is important to be married—especially, for women. Engagement itself seems to hold a sacred position. If we break an engagement we are seen as insincere or untrustworthy. While "breech of promise" is no longer a legal issue, a certain stigma remains about breaking engagements. Thus, there may be many subtle pressures on young people to marry, and those pressures can become much less subtle when two people are engaged.

Natalie and Drew had problems from the beginning of their courtship. In the early days, Natalie had pursued Drew, as he was very shy and insecure. Drew was flattered by Natalie's attention. They dated and were eventually engaged. Being desired by someone else and having the improved social status that engagement brought increased Drew's self-esteem and self-confidence. Now he found it easy to talk to women. When several single women, whom he previously had thought were out of his league, began to pay attention to him, he reevaluated his situation and concluded that while he appreciated many of Natalie's qualities, and was grateful that she had brought him out of his shell, he did not love her. When he realized his feelings, he told her he wanted to date other people.

Natalie became upset, threatened suicide, and told their pastor what her boyfriend was doing. The pastor told Drew he was obligated to marry her because he was violating a commitment if he didn't. This, in addition to social criticism and guilt regarding his fiancee's pain, led Drew to the marriage altar. Later, the same pressures that wouldn't let him out of the engagement were even stronger in not letting him out of the marriage. If Drew (and the pastor) had had a different definition of commitment, the marriage might not have taken place.

LEVELS OF COMMITMENT

We are distressed by a society which takes commitment so lightly. Commitments should be honored. However, commitment is not an all-or-nothing concept. There are degrees of commitment and these degrees depend on the context of the situation. We will examine the definitions of commitment as they are applied to the various levels of relationships.

Casual dating commitment. the couple that is dating has a commitment for a certain period of time, for example, Friday night from seven to eleven-thirty. During that time they focus their attention on each other and treat each other respectfully. After the date is over, each will speak well of the other. There is no commitment for the future.

Exclusive dating commitment. the couple has a dating commitment for an indefinite period. During the times they are together they focus on one another and treat each other respectfully. When they are not with each other they speak well of each other. Each agrees not to date other people during the time of this agreement. The agreement can be broken by one person's saying he or she no longer wishes to date the other exclusively. The agreement is verbally terminated before dating other persons takes place.

Engagement commitment. the couple involved has a "tentatively" permanent time commitment. It is tentative because engagement is a trial period. It is as if one person were saying to the other, "I love you and want to marry you. I'm through exploring other relationships and wish to develop a relationship with you. I believe you are the person with whom I wish to spend the rest of my life. If things work out the way I think and want them to, and if I continue to feel about you the way I do now, I will want to marry you."

Each agrees to not date other people during the term of engagement. The engagement can be broken by one person saying he or she no longer wishes to be engaged. The relationship can be terminated unilaterally or mutually renegotiated to a different level of commitment.

Marriage commitment. the commitment is permanent. The man and woman are saying to each other: "I am not free to leave the marriage because I am unhappy or wish to be with someone else. If we have difficulties, I will work with you to resolve the problem."

The definition of commitment, regardless of the level, is useful only if both people share the same definition. If one partner has a different definition, someone is likely to be hurt. If both are using the definition for *marriage* (permanent commitment) but they have just recently become *engaged,* they could be trapping themselves in an undesirable relationship.

We want to emphasize the importance of the trial aspect of engagement. It is not a trial in the sense, "I don't think I love you, but let's get engaged and see how it goes for a while. Maybe being engaged will change my feelings." It is a trial in the sense, "I love you very much and can't imagine not loving you. But marriage is very important—it's permanent. I want to make sure we both continue feeling the way we do now. If we get through the next six months and we are still feeling the same, then let's put the final touches on our wedding plans."

Obviously, this is a very mature statement for an engaged person to make. Even if the couple doesn't volunteer this kind of statement on their own, the pastor can share this definition with the couple.

By accepting the Engagement Commitment definition, the engagement period can be a time of relationship growth and yet offer an escape option if one or both of the people begin to have doubts.

LENGTH OF ENGAGEMENT

How long does the engagement need to be? If it is a trial period and marriage is permanent, wouldn't a longer engagement be better?

Times have changed. Long engagements are no longer in vogue. In fact, data suggests that couples who are engaged (formally or informally) for three years or longer, often do not end up marrying. We don't know why this is true. It may be that the lack of intense love leads to the protracted dating or engagement with the hope that strong love will emerge in time. Regardless, a long engagement usually doesn't produce love, if that kind of love doesn't emerge early in the relationship.

When is the length of engagement and/or exclusive dating not long enough? The important factor is not the length of time per se, but the intensity of the relationship, the frequency of times together, and the duration of time. Harold Bessell's research on romance describes the importance of distinguishing true romantic (enduring) love from infatuation (short term). Unfortunately, romantic love and infatuation cannot be easily distinguished at the beginning of the relationship.[1]

Bessell believes that a couple needs to spend intense time together—four out of five workday evenings, and half of the weekend, for a period of three months. That is the *maximum* intensity. If the couple still feels the same romantic feelings of attraction as they did at the beginning, they are probably experiencing true romantic love.

It makes sense to encourage couples to spend as much time together as they can without neglecting their families, churches, friends, and personal hobbies. For most couples, at least six months of relatively heavy dating makes sense. When people are busy with work, school, church, sports or hobbies, a year at the Engagement Commitment level would not be too long. With younger couples, in their teens or early twenties, we suggest an even longer time.

Bessell writes from a secular perspective, but he does not advise a man and woman to live together. Even though he supports high-intensity relationships, he believes cohabitation only makes it more difficult to separate infatuation from true love.

MATE SELECTION

Social psychologists have developed theories regarding some of the selection variables. Levinger and Snoek have identified four stages of relationship: zero contact, awareness, surface contact, and mutuality.[2] *Zero contact* occurs when people are around us, but we have no relationship with them. *Awareness* occurs when we become aware of another person because of observable positive external characteristics. This stage is powerfully influenced by physical attractiveness, status symbols, or trappings of success. The next stage, *surface contact*, occurs when we meet the person and begin a social relationship. This is where the exploring of surface issues takes place. As we find out about hobbies, interests, and likes and dislikes, we will reinforce each other if we like each other. This reinforcement is necessary for the relationship to continue. If it does, we enter the attitude similarity substage where we begin to explore some deeper issues by exposing attitudes, beliefs, and values. If these are similar, the feelings of liking one another will increase and we will feel closer. The last stage is *mutuality*. At this stage, we begin to explore the possibility of putting our two lives together.

Murstein's stimulus-value-role theory supports the ideas of Levinger and Snoek while adding dimensions of his own.[3] In the *stimulus* stage, at the beginning of the relationship, physical appearance and status symbols attract one person to another. This is similar to the awareness stage referred to earlier. The second stage, *value comparison*, has to do with interests, beliefs, and attitudes. This is similar to the attitude similarity substage of surface contact. The *role* stage occurs when the couple behaviorally carries out their beliefs, values, attitudes, and interests. Sometimes couples experience conflict at the role stage but have a tendency to ignore the warning signs. A fallacious belief that things will change for the better is often held. Regardless of whose theory is used, Waring points out that couples who have problems later in marriage have not adequately explored attitudes, values, beliefs, and needs, nor have they engaged in self-disclosure during courtship.[4]

COLLUSION DURING THE PREMARRIAGE PERIOD

An informal research project was done at the University of Nebraska in 1975, with approximately forty engaged couples attending a Catholic Pre-Cana workshop. They completed an inventory designed to tap into individual values, attitudes, and beliefs and while doing so, the couples were allowed to sit together. At the following month's Pre-Cana, a similar sized group of engaged couples completed the same inventory. For this administration, however, the men completed their inventories in one room, while the women completed theirs in another room.

The results from the two groups were compared. For the group of men and women who sat together while completing the inventory, their agreement scores were very close. These couples appeared to be very compatible. In the other group, however, the agreement factor was much more varied. Some couples appeared to be very much in agreement—very compatible—while other couples had little agreement.

The researchers reached two conclusions: (a) couples during courtship often keep from disclosing information that might emphasize dissimilarity and (b) couples during courtship focus on, and even overemphasize, areas of similarity. This process of information control does not appear to be a conscious attempt to delude one another, but is more of an unconscious attempt to keep the romantic boat from rocking. They seem to engage in a kind of feedback process in which one checks out the other, and vice versa, to arrive at a consensus.

We describe four types of non-self-disclosures: (a) accidental, (b) love conquers all, (c) "I need to look good," and (d) "we can work on it later."

Accidental non-self-disclosure. Issues that might be a problem in the marriage are bypassed unintentionally. The couple who are young, coming to their first marriage, with a short dating/engagement period and no premarriage counseling, and whose families are disinterested are likely to overlook many important issues. They lack life experiences and outside stimuli to help them consider the various issues. As a result, less disclosure will occur.

Love conquers all non-self-disclosure. The persons are aware that something bothers them, but they minimize its importance. A young man, who has gone duck hunting with his father and brothers for years, thinks he has outgrown hunting after repeatedly hearing his fiancee speak disparagingly of it. A woman who values total abstinence begins to accept social drinking when her fiance and his family seem casual and comfortable around alcohol.

The changes in values and behaviors are likely to receive greater acceptance from the fiance, his family and friends. These changes are not coerced; there is not a demand to "stop hunting" or "start drinking." The changed person usually explains the change as, "I've outgrown that," or "it just doesn't interest me the way it used to."

These changes are usually temporary. If we liked country music before falling in love, we will like it afterwards—even if our fiance is a classical violinist. If we usually slept in late Sunday mornings and then watched a football game, we will probably do the same after the wedding. This is true even after attending church together for the two months of courtship.

This is not to say the changes that took place can't last. However, we need to look for a very good reason why they should. A religious conversion experience would predict a permanent change in church-attendance habits. Falling in love with the pastor's daughter doesn't.

I need to look good non-self-disclosure. These behaviors are similar to the preceding ones, but are more consciously practiced. They have to do with weaknesses people know they have. People improve manners, lose weight, stop smoking, stop drinking, or start making more ambitious vocational and educational plans, because they want to make a good impression.

These behaviors often occur very early in the relationship. Social desirability is the key. We put on that mask that is going to make us acceptable to the most people, and this charade continues during the courtship and doesn't begin to erode until after the marriage.

We can work it out later non-self-disclosure. This is the most

211

obvious case of self-deception. Here we are aware of the problem, but we don't want to accept it as it is. In fact, we plan to change it. We are deluded by a false belief, "it will be easier to change later than it is now."

DISCLOSURE OF EXPECTATIONS

The theoretical orientation of the previous section comes from social psychology literature. Another contributor, Sager, who voices more of a psychodynamic and systems point of view, believes that all relationships are contractual.[5] "I will do thus and so for you, if you do thus and so for me. If you don't come through for me, I won't come through for you." In chapter 3, in the example of George and Marti, the snowballing effect of a tit-for-tat interaction was described. George did not expect Marti's dad to live with them after they were married, but Marti did. Marti did not plan to work after they were married, but George assumed she would. After Marti quit work and her dad moved in with them, George's behavior became more negative toward Marti. In reaction to George's negative change, Marti withdrew some of her positive behaviors from George.

Sager says the expectations we have for one another appear on three levels. The first level is conscious-verbalized, the second is conscious-unverbalized, and the third level is unconscious-unverbalized. The conscious-verbalized level presents no problem because these expectations are shared. At the other extreme, the unconscious-unverbalized material requires many counseling sessions. It is somewhat easier for the counselor to help the couple work through the conscious-unverbalized level.

The reasons for not verbalizing expectations include all those described by the social psychologists, such as not wanting to rock the romantic boat, believing it will be easier to work out problems after the wedding, wanting to put the best foot forward or "I think I've really changed my values since I met my intended."

Sager's research suggests additional reasons. For example, one person may assume that the other will do things a certain way. He or she thinks, "after all, doesn't everyone do it this way?" If your family spends all the holidays together, isn't it natural to expect that all families do the same thing?

Another reason for not talking about an issue is fear of embarrassment. The thought is, *I would like you to do* _____ *(fill in the blank) but I'm embarrassed to ask for it or discuss it. I just hope that after we are married, it turns out that you and I feel the same way about this.*

IMPLEMENTING PREMARITAL SELF-DISCLOSURE

At least four factors can contribute to premarital self-disclosure. Two are in the direct control of the couple and two are orchestrated by the counselor.

A year-long engagement. This is not an arbitrary, twelve-month engagement period. Rather, it considers the elements discussed about engagement in the earlier part of the chapter. The actual length of time the diamond is on the fourth finger of the left hand is immaterial. The important issues are how committed and how intense the relationship has been. Most couples, in this busy society of ours, need from nine to twelve months of committed shared social activity to get to know each other well.

Varied activities. Two couples, both engaged for the same period of time and having the same amount of contact may enter marriage with very different levels of knowledge about each other. A couple who spends all of its time doing the same thing will know far less about each other than the couple who is continually participating in varying activities. Traveling, meeting a variety of people, being a part of different social organizations, and participating in several recreational activities will bring out different sides of each person's personality. The more sides of the personality that are brought out together, the better.

Premarriage counseling personality-trait assessment. In this phase of counseling, each person is given one or several tests of personality. These tests are taken individually, not as a couple. The Taylor-Johnson Temperament Analysis, Minnesota Multiphasic Personality Inventory, or Myers-Briggs Type Indicator could be used.

The purpose of the personality testing is twofold: It enables the counselor to do matching and it forces self-disclosure.

To do matching, the counselor looks for those traits in each person that go together. If, for example, each person in the couple was found to have a need to both give and receive attention, that would be a good match. On the other hand, if one or both had a strong need to receive attention but didn't like to give it, that would be a poor match.

While the couple may not have the skills to determine which personality traits go well together, each person knows what he or she likes. The counselor reviews the personality tests and each person gets a clearer peek at the other.

Premarriage counseling: personal and marital issues assessment. This part of premarriage assessment explores the areas that make up day-to-day living.

We have developed an instrument for this purpose: the Marital Success Development Inventory (MSDI).[6] It asks each person to state how he or she feels about twenty questions in each of the following areas: communication, roles, sex and love, personality, social life, religious and social values, finances, in-laws, children, and recreational activities. Next, each person states how he or she would feel if the other partner were to hold the opposite point of view. If he or she can easily accept the partner feeling differently, this item is of minor importance. If the opposite point of view is bothersome but tolerable, it is of moderate importance. If the answer is disapproved of, it is of major importance. Lastly, each person guesses how the other will actually answer the question.

The MSDI gives the couple, with the aid of the counselor, some very practical information. Each person is asked to go on record as to what is actually believed and how strongly. They also must consider how strong the reaction would be if the partner were to hold a contrary position. Information of this sort frequently doesn't surface until after the wedding.

Another instrument, designed for the same purpose as the MSDI, is Prepare-Enrich. *Prepare* is designed to be used in premarriage counseling and *Enrich* is designed for marriage counseling. Both of these are computer-scored inventories that are available to pastoral counselors.[7]

In addition, a needs or expectations assessment could be done. Even though Willard Harley's book, *His Needs, Her Needs,* is aimed at married couples, the engaged couple would benefit from completing his Marital Needs Questionnaire.[8] It is our belief that the sooner a couple can understand each other's needs and work toward meeting those needs, the greater the chance the marriage has for enduring.

Several workbooks are available that can help the couple uncover nonverbalized expectations or needs. These work best if they are used in a structured setting. Answering and discussing the issues raised by every section of the workbook is essential to present avoidance of trouble spots. Two workbooks to consider are *How Can I Be Sure* and *Before You Say "I Do."*[9]

Pre-remarriage counseling also involves some unique issues that need to be addressed. Some of these are grieving and closing the past, children and stepparenting, relationships to outsiders, and legal matters. *Remarriage: Challenge and Opportunity* (pastor's reference) by Peter L. Velander is a helpful available resource.[10]

CHANGING EXPECTATIONS

Some couples are afraid of premarriage counseling because they fear the pastor is going to talk them out of getting married. In some cases this may be true. If there are major differences in personality, values, attitudes, and beliefs, the counselor may advise the couple to select partners who are more compatible. Most of the premarital couples we counsel have important differences, but these differences are not major enough to preclude a successful marriage.

Minor differences can often be handled by changing expectations. This example is sometimes used.

Dwayne is car shopping. He is interested in good gas mileage. He currently drives a pre-oil-embargo car which gets 12 miles per gallon. The sticker on the car he is looking at says he can expect 32 miles per gallon. Upon asking the salesperson if that is accurate, he is told that the figure is too optimistic, but that he can expect about 27 or 28 mpg. Dwayne is initially disappointed. But he likes the car in all other respects and decides that 27 or 28 mpg is a lot better than the 12 he is currently getting, so he buys the new car. After it is broken in he checks the mileage. He gets 27.4 mpg. Why is Dwayne happy?

215

Most everyone agrees that Dwayne is happy because the car met his expectations. We then ask, "What would Dwayne be feeling if he hadn't asked about the mileage and thought he was going to get 32 mpg?" Most agree he would be unhappy because the car would not have lived up to his expectations.

Persons gain power by getting all (or as much as possible) of the available information before making a decision. If their information is complete and valid and they decide they can live with the outcome, they will usually make the decision in that direction. The very same condition that could have been accepted with foreknowledge, becomes a point of contention if it isn't known about until later.

Knowing about a partner's differences will not usually affect the decision to marry as long as those differences are minor. If they are major, the issue is different . For example, if the salesperson had told Dwayne the car only got twenty mpg, Dwayne would have decided against the car. The difference between twenty and thirty-two is too great.

COMBINING GROUP AND INDIVIDUAL COUNSELING

Premarriage counseling creates another demand on the pastor's time. While some premarital programs are excellent, others are shallow. Many pastors have time to give three or four individual sessions. If a couple is seen for just four sessions, half of the time is spent in getting acquainted and arranging the wedding details. We would like to see more time allocated to substantive content areas.

The pastor may be able to mix group activities with individual couple work. One of the goals in premarital counseling is for each person to disclose herself or himself to the other; whether this happens in a group of ten other couples or alone in the pastor's office is immaterial.

Some individual couple counseling time is necessary, especially for the less mature or less sophisticated couple. The counselor may need to highlight some areas of differences and conflict so the couple will be forced to confront them. If couples meet only in groups, some will not be challenged to reevaluate their relationship.

Important information and relational tools and techniques for use in marriage can effectively be presented to the engaged couple in a group setting. Subject matter such as communication models, roles, sexual information, handling of finances, and dealing with in-laws can be presented to a group just as well as in one-on-one counseling.

The use of groups in premarriage is not only time efficient; it also provides an opportunity for engaged couples to benefit from one another's questions and perspectives.

As efficient as groups are, they are not a substitute for individual work. Individual time must be utilized to address the unique issues each couple brings.

If a pastor works with four couples at a time, and mixes five group sessions with three individual sessions with each couple, the total group can be seen in seventeen sessions. If the mix were two individual sessions and six group sessions, it would only take fourteen sessions to work with four couples. This compares with sixteen sessions that would be required to see four couples for four sessions each, on an individual basis. If a pastor does not have enough couples at one time to run a group, several churches combined can make group premarriage counseling feasible.

Since one of the goals in premarriage counseling is to expose one person to the other and to give each one time to digest the information, it makes sense to see a couple for eight sessions over a two- to three-month period rather than once a week for a month. Although we have done all-day premarriage workshops, we believe that spreading the counseling sessions out will come closer to reaching your counseling goals.

The group approach provides an efficient way to deal with premarriage information. In addition, several couples tend to bring up issues that might not be raised by the pastor alone.

Summary

The key element at the premarriage level is selection. At this time, each person should identify important traits for a life partner. Then, the engaged person should check to see whether the potential partner does, in fact, have those traits. Unfortunately, this is the very time when deeper beliefs, values, attitudes, needs, and expectations are frequently hidden from view.

We have discussed the importance of self-disclosure in the mate selection process. Premarriage counseling may be expanded to include assessment of personality, using an instrument like the Taylor-Johnson Temperament Analysis (TJTA), and assessment of personal and marital issues, using an instrument like the Marital Success Development Inventory (MSDI). We also recommend lengthening the number of premarriage counseling sessions to eight and including some group work.

EPILOGUE

A PERSONAL WORD FROM
THE AUTHORS

Someone once said that happiness is not a destination; it is a way of traveling. Just when you think you have a handle on things, something new comes along. It can probably also be said that the essence of living is discovery.

Discovery brings happiness. A successful marriage includes the happiness of discovering the changes in my partner and myself as we relate to life stages and life events.

"While Dee was in graduate school," says Ruby, "I thought, 'when we are finished with school, then life will begin.' Afterwards I discovered it had already begun, and I had missed some of the adventure and excitement of being in graduate school. I also discovered that other portions of my life were perceived through that 'wait until' attitude. Thinking of the 'wait until' attitude makes me sad because of what I missed. Fortunately, I'm able to change that old attitude to one that takes joy in discovering what is new and what is wonderful about today."

When we think about marriage, we think about working as hard as one can to apply principles that will strengthen the marriage. If both partners are committed to making it work, we believe most marriages can work. Working on a marriage also involves commitment to discovery. We need to discover our partner's needs. At the same time we need to be open with our partner to enable him or her to discover our needs. It is useful to remember why we wished to marry in the first place—to *share* our lives with someone we love.

Being a counselor also involves discovery. Doing marriage counseling requires a willingness to enter the process of discovery with a couple. What will work for this couple? How will they deal with their issues? It is often hard, but, it is rewarding work.

Another important area of discovery for the counselor is that of the counseling process itself. Counselors must continue to learn and be open to new ideas in order to better serve their clients. We do not take lightly the task of entering into couple's lives. It is a privilege, and we enter carefully and prayerfully. We hope that this book will help you to do the same.

Dee and Ruby Friesen

APPENDIX 1

PREAMBLE FOR MARRIAGE

WE BELIEVE—healthy marriages evolve from individuals who are working at personal fulfillment and the development of inner peace.

Personal fulfillment includes gaining insight into one's motivations, needs, and desires. Inner peace is the development of one's personal relationship with God. Both of these lead to positive self-esteem.

WE BELIEVE—humans should have respect for others, and especially for one's spouse.

Each person is created in God's image with his or her own set of characteristics, abilities, needs, and desires. These unique qualities do not make one person superior or inferior, but each must learn how to live with, cope with, and handle the unique qualities of the other in a nonjudgmental way.

For example, my (Ruby speaking) thinking style is sequential. That is, for me, it feels most comfortable to deal with step one and then go on to step two. My husband's natural thinking style is more random. He starts at step one but quickly sidetracks to related issues. Thus, when I ask a question requiring a simple answer, he gives me the reason behind the answer, not a simple yes or no. There is potential for frustration from my feeling he hasn't answered the question and from his feeling that he has. When we came to understand this difference in our thinking styles, we began to respect the qualities of each. This example underscores the need for both understanding and acceptance. One may not always precede the other, but acceptance usually is easier if one first gains understanding.

WE BELIEVE—Christian marriages grow when there is a mutual understanding and acceptance in a nonjudgmental atmosphere.

WE BELIEVE—that an issue which is a problem for one partner is really a problem for both partners.

All too often we hear, "This is not my problem; this is his or her problem." Being yoked together is a biblical metaphor for the Christian marriage. What affects one member of a yoked team automatically affects the other.

WE BELIEVE—each person must be willing to change or adjust within the limits of his or her personal integrity and ability.

WE BELIEVE—one partner must tell the other how he or she feels, must ask for what he or she wants, and must be willing to assist with change.

This is a willingness to be open and honest as best we can, without being destructive. In our view, this level of commitment is embodied in the Christian marriage contract or vows. Included is a commitment to gain insight, to develop skills, and to take long-term action that will create an environment that fosters maturity and attainment of full potential.

WE BELIEVE—these values are consistent with Christ's admonition in Matthew 7:12: "In everything, do to others what you would have them do to you, for this sums up the Law and the Prophets."

And to Paul's words found in Ephesians 5:21–28: "Submit to one another out of reverence for Christ. Wives, submit to your husbands as to the Lord. For the husband is the head of the wife as Christ is the head of the church, his body, of which he is the Savior. Now as the church submits to Christ, so also wives should submit to their husbands in everything. Husbands, love your wives, just as Christ loved the church and gave himself up for her to make her holy, cleansing her by the washing with water through the word, and to present her to himself as a radiant church, without stain or wrinkle or any other blemish, but holy and blameless. In this same way, husbands ought to love their wives as their own bodies. He who loves his wife loves himself."

COUPLE "FEELING" WORD ACTIVITY

Larry Day, Ph.D.

Directions: Listed on page 225 are feeling words. Please fill in the first blank with feeling words selected from this list or others you like. Then complete the sentence stem (second blank) according to what would be meaningful for you. Verbally share this with your partner. For example, "I feel <u>accepted</u> when <u>you listen to me</u>."

accepted	confident	important	restricted
accused	courageous	inadequate	satisfied
affectionate	committed	influential	seductive
afraid	crushed	insincere	sexual
aimless	delighted	intimidated	sorrowful
alarmed	depressed	joyful	special
alienated	dignity	judgmental	surprised
alive	eager	liberated	supported
ambitious	encouraged	loved	tender
ambivalent	excited	lustful	thankful
amused	exhausted	natural	threatened
angry	flirtatious	nervous	torn
annoyed	forgiving	noble	understood
anxious	free	optimistic	unique
appreciated	frustrated	outraged	uplifted
apprehensive	generous	panicky	valued
burdened	grateful	passionate	virtuous
burned up	guilty	protective	vulnerable
cheated	happy	proud	wonderful
closed up	helpless	rebellious	worried
condemned	hopeful	refreshed	worthwhile

APPENDIX 3

CONFIDENTIAL DATA INVENTORY

(print or write clearly)

Date _____

Name _____ Phone (home) _____

Address _____ Phone (work) _____

City, State _____ Zip _____

Male _____ Female _____ Race _____ Age _____ Date of birth _____

Place of birth _____

Referred by _____ Family Doctor _____

Living Arrangements: Own _____ Rent _____ Other (explain) _____

How long at present address? _____ Number of addresses in last 10 years. _____

Do you have any serious financial problems?   No _____ Yes _____

If yes, explain. _____

Please fill in the blanks:

	Counselee	Spouse
Employer		
Job Title		
Years at this job		

Personal Data

Individual History

Are you adopted? _____ If yes, describe the circumstances:

When _____

Where _____

By whom _____

What age _____

When you were born, were there any medical or emotional complications for you or your mother? _____ If yes, explain.
_____

List all serious diseases or illnesses you had as a child or teenager (include age). _____
_____

List all serious operations or accidents that you had as a child and state your age at the time. _____
_____

Please describe any fearful or distressing experiences not previously mentioned. _____
_____

Describe your earliest memory. _____
_____

Medical History

List all serious illnesses, operations, injuries, and hospitalizations not previously mentioned. (Give dates and treatment). _____

_____

List all current medication and reason for taking. _____

_____

Are there any hereditary diseases in your family? _____

What physical impairments, scars, or disfigurements do you have?

_____

Have you ever had venereal disease? _____ If yes, explain. _____

_____

List past psychiatric treatment or hospitalization (when, where, how long, and who treated you).

_____

Have you ever taken medication for emotional problems? _____
If yes, explain. (what, when, and for how long) _____

_____

Have you had suicidal ideas? _____ Ever attempted suicide? _____
Do you think you would? _____

Height _____ Weight _____

Any recent change in weight? _____ If yes, explain.

_____

Date of last physical:

Checkup _____ Why _____ Results _____

Have you had problems with:

Compulsive eating _____ Nervous eating _____ Inability to eat _____

Marital History

Marital status _____ Date of marriage _____

How long did you know your spouse before marriage? _____

Did you engage in premarital sex? _____ Were you pregnant at the time of marriage? _____

Is your sex life with your spouse satisfactory? _____ If no, explain. _____

Have you been married previously? ____ If yes, when and how long were you married, and how did it end? _____

Have there ever been any threats of violence from your spouse? ____ If yes, explain. _____

Has there been actual violence? ____ If yes, explain. _____
_____

How are conflicts handled within your marriage? _____
_____

How did your parents handle conflicts within their marriage? ____
_____

Do you have any problems with marital communication? _____ If yes, please elaborate. _____

Please describe your parents' communication style. _____
_____

How is love and caring displayed in your marriage by you? _____
_____

By your spouse. _____

How was love and caring displayed in your parent's marriage? ____
_____

Are you satisfied with your marriage? _____ If not, explain and state how it could be improved. _____

General Sexual History

What were your parents' attitude towards sex? Was there sex instruction or discussion at home? _____

When and how did you first learn about sex? _____
_____

Are you or have you been sexually active outside of a marriage relationship? _____

Have you ever had a homosexual experience? _____

Have you ever been molested or abused? _____

Have you ever had an unusual, unpleasant, or frightening sexual experience? _____ If yes, explain. _____

In my opinion, sex is: _____

229

Sexual History (women)

Age of onset of periods _____ Were you prepared?_____
____ yes ____ no. If not, explain. _____

Do you experience any menstrual pain or irregularity? __ yes __ no

Do periods affect your mood? _____ If yes, explain. _____
_____

Have there been any complications during or following your pregnancies? _____

If yes, explain. _____

Have you ever had a miscarriage? _____ If yes, what and when was your emotional reaction. _____

Have you ever had an abortion? _____ If yes, what and when was your emotional reaction. _____

Have you or are you about to experience menopause? _____ If yes, how has it affected you? _____

How did your mother's menopause affect you? _____
_____

How did your mother's menopause affect her? _____
_____

Family History

Has or does a member of your family suffer from a mental disturbance? _____

If yes, what is the nature of the illness? _____

If yes, has this resulted in hospitalization and/or treatment? _____

Have you ever lost a member of your family or someone close to you through death? _____ If yes, whom did you lose, how old were you at the time, how did this person die, and how did you react? _____
_____

Among the members of my family listed earlier:

I feel closest to _____

I feel least close to _____

List any people who were not listed on the preceding page that are living in your house. Give names, ages, relation, and reason for being in your house. _____

The person who has had the greatest influence on my life is _____

Why? _____

What was home like? _____

Were you able to confide in your parents? __ yes __ no

Home was: very happy ____ happy ____ okay ____ unhappy ____ very unhappy ____

In what ways were you punished? _____

Were your parents divorced or separated? ____ If yes, how old were you, what were the circumstances, and how did you react? _____

Why did the divorce or separation occur? _____

With which parent did you live? _____

Did this parent remarry? _____ If yes, how old were you? _____

Mark an *x* on each line at the approximate point that most closely describes your feelings.

My father was   1   2   3   4   5

Strong . . . . Weak

Warm . . . . Cold

Close . . . . Distant

Happy . . . . Sad

Good . . . . Bad

Interested . . . . Uninterested

Smart . . . . Stupid

Loving .... Hateful

Masculine .... Feminine

Industrious .... Lazy

Generous .... Stingy

Healthy .... Sick

Accepting .... Critical

Strict .... Lax

Rich .... Poor

My mother was   1   2   3   4   5

Strong .... Weak

Warm .... Cold

Close .... Distant

Happy .... Sad

Good .... Bad

Interested .... Uninterested

Smart .... Stupid

Loving .... Hateful

Feminine .... Masculine

Industrious .... Lazy

Generous .... Stingy

Healthy .... Sick

Accepting .... Critical

Strict .... Lax

Rich .... Poor

My parents were: Excellent parents _____ Good parents _____
Okay parents _____ Poor parents _____ Very poor parents _____

I was closest to: Mother _____ Father _____ Same _____

My parents were: Very strict _____ Strict _____ Moderate _____
Not Strict _____ Didn't care _____

Compared to my brothers and sisters, my parents punished me:
More _____ Less _____ Same _____

School History

Age started _____ Last grade and age completed _____

Number of different grammar schools attended _____

Were you ever: _____ in special classes _____ often truant

Did you have any special difficulties or problems in school? _____
If yes, explain. _____

School Participation

Athletics: Active _____ Average _____ Less than average _____
None _____

Grades: Honor roll _____ Above average _____ Average _____

Popularity: Very popular _____ Popular _____ Average _____
Unpopular _____ Very unpopular _____ Loner _____

Dating: Very Much _____ Much _____ Average _____ Little _____
Very little _____ None _____

Age of first date: _____

Occupational History

Number of jobs in past 10 years _____ Ever fired? _____
If yes, explain. _____

What job have you held longest, and for how long? _____

Number of promotions in the last 5 years _____ Do you want to
be promoted? _____

Are you satisfied with your current job? _____ If not, explain. _____

Religion

Your religion _____ Spouse's _____

COUNSELING AND MARRIAGE

Has either of you changed religions? _____ If yes, why? _____

Your church _____

Attend services: Regularly _____ Occasionally _____ Never _____

I am devout _____ I believe, but am not devout _____ I feel hypocritical _____

I am ready to give up _____ I have given up _____

Parent's religion: Mother _____ Father _____

Have there been marked changes in your religious beliefs? _____
If yes, explain. _____

Hobbies

List your chief interest and hobbies. _____

Have there been any changes in your interest or involvement in these activities. _____ If yes, explain. _____ How is most of your free time occupied? _____

Do you have enough free time? _____

Alcohol and Drug Use

I drink: Heavily ___ Moderately ___ Occasionally ___ Never ___

Have you ever used drugs? _____ If yes, which drugs and how long? _____

Does use of above items interfere with your home life, social life, work, or school life? _____ If yes, explain. _____

NOTES

Chapter 1 Beginning with the Counselor

1. Patricia Gundry, *Heirs Together* (Grand Rapids: Zondervan Publishing House, 1980).
2. Robbie Joy, "Making Our Marriage Work," *Virtue* 10 (1988): 21–23.
3. Gordon McMinn, "Spiritual Gifts Inventory" (201 Jefferson Bldg., 9370 S.W. Greenburg Rd., Portland, Ore. 97223, 1975).

Chapter 2 Beginning with the Counselee

1. Richard B. Stuart, *Helping Couples Change* (New York: Guilford Press, 1980).

Chapter 3 Individual Approach vs. Systems Approach

1. Jay Haley, *Problem Solving Therapy* (San Francisco: Jossey-Bass, 1987), 161–62.
2. Luigi Boscolo, Gianfranco Cecchin, Lynn Hoffman, and Peggy Penn, *Milan Systemic Family Therapy* (New York: Basic Books, 1987), 5.

3. Jordan Paul and Margaret Paul, *Do I Have to Give Up Me to Be Loved by You?* (Minneapolis: CompCare Publications, 1983).

4. David Viscott, *I Love You, Let's Work It Out* (New York: Simon and Schuster, 1987).

5. Ellen Bader and Peter Pearson, "The Developmental Stages of Couplehood" (The Couples Institute, 445 Burgess Drive, Menlo Park, Calif. 94025, 1987).

6. James Dobson, "Turn Your Heart Toward Home" (Focus on the Family, P.O. Box, Pomona, Calif. 91769, 1986).

7. Clifford Sager, *Marriage Contracts and Couple Therapy* (New York: Brunner-Mazel, 1976).

8. Willard Harley, *His Needs, Her Needs* (Old Tappan, N.J.: Fleming H. Revell, 1986).

Chapter 4 Setting the Structure for Hope

1. Rueben Hill, *Families under Stress* (New York: Harper and Brothers, 1949).

2. DeLoss Friesen, "Divorce Proofing Your Marriage" (Video Series, East-West Video, Brush Prairie, Wash., 1982).

Chapter 5 What Next? Decision Strategies for the Counselor

1. Harvey Ruben, *Super Marriage: Overcoming the Predictable Crises of Married Life* (New York: Bantam Books, 1986), 250.

2. Paul Meehl, Clinical versus Statistical Prediction (Minneapolis: University of Minnesota Press, 1954), 119.

3. S. R. Hathaway and J. C. McKinley, *Minnesota Multiphasic Personality Inventory* (Minneapolis: University Press, 1982).

4. Theodore Millon, *Millon Clinical Multiaxial Inventory* (Minneapolis: National Computer Systems, 1984).

5. Katharine Briggs and Isabel Briggs Myers, *Myers-Briggs Type Indicator* (Palo Alto, Calif.: Consulting Psychologists Press, 1976).

6. Taylor and Johnson, *Taylor-Johnson Temperament Analysis* (Los Angeles: Psychological Publications, 1985).

7. H. J. Locke, and K. M. Wallace, "Short Marital-Adjustment and Prediction Tests: Their Reliability and Validity," *Marriage and Family Living* (1959): 251–55.

8. Richard Stuart and Frieda Stuart, *Marital Pre-Counseling Inventory* (Champaign, Ill.: Research Press, 1973).

9. Richard Stuart and Barbara Jacobson, *Couple's Therapy Workbook* (Champaign, Ill.: Research Press, 1983).

10. DeLoss Friesen, "Marriage Success Development Inventory" (6485 Palomino Way, West Linn, Ore. 97068, rev. 1988).

11. Arnold Lazarus, *Multimodal Life History Questionnaire* (Champaign, Ill.: Research Press, 1980).

12. Willard Harley, *His Needs, Her Needs* (Old Tappan, N.J.: Fleming H. Revell, 1986).

13. Paul Hauck, *Three Faces of Love* (Philadelphia: Westminster Press, 1984).

Chapter 6 The Marital Pyramid and the Place of Communication

1. P. Bornstein and M. Bornstein, *Marital Therapy: A Behavior Communication Approach* (New York: Pergamon Press, 1986).

2. Julian Fast, *Body Language* (New York: Pocket Books, 1971).

3. Ricks Warren and Terri Warren, *Tender Talk* (Portland, Ore.: Portland Press, 1985).

4. J. Gottman, C. Notarius, J. Gonso, J. and H. Markman, *A Couple's Guide to Communication* (Champaign, Ill.: Research Press, 1976).

Chapter 7 Conflict Management: "Don't Let the Sun Go Down on Your Wrath"

1. B. Kantrowitz, with P. Winget in Washington, D.C., J. Gordon in Los Angeles, R. Michael and D. Witherspoon in New York, E. Calonius and D. L. Gonzales in Miami, and B. Turgue in Detroit, "How to Stay Married," *Newsweek*, 24 August 1987, 52–57.

2. David Viscott, *I Love You, Let's Work It Out* (New York: Simon and Schuster, 1987), 20–42.

3. Paul Tournier, *To Understand Each Other* (Richmond, Va.: John Knox Press, 1962), 8, 17.

4. Jordan Paul and Margaret Paul, *Do I Have to Give Up Me to Be Loved by You* (Minneapolis: CompCare Publications, 1983), 12.

5. Robert E. Alberti and Michael L. Emmonds, *Your Perfect Right*, rev. ed. (San Luis Obispo, Calif.: Impact Publishers, 1986). John Faul and David Augsburger, *Beyond Assertiveness* (Waco, Tex.: Calibre/Word, 1980).

6. Robert Weiss, *Modality Check* (Eugene, Ore.: University of Oregon Press, n.d.).

7. Lisa Engelhardt, "The Ten Commandments for Fighting Fair," *Catholic Update* (January 1988): 1–2, 1615 Republic Street, Cincinnati, OH 45210.

8. L. H. Goldhor, *The Dance of Anger: A Woman's Guide to Changing Patterns of Intimate Relationships* (New York: Harper and Row, 1985).

9. Edward Wheat, *How to Save Your Marriage Alone* (Grand Rapids: Zondervan, 1983).

10. Thomas Gordon, *Parent Effectiveness Training* (New York: Peter H. Wyden, 1970), 49–94.

11. David Keirsey and Marilyn Bates, *Please Understand Me: Character and Temperament Types* (Del Mar, Calif.: Prometheus Nemesis Books, 1978), 1.

Chapter 8 Helping Your Clients Tell Themselves the Truth

1. Albert Ellis, *Reason and Emotion in Psychotherapy* (Secaucus, N.J.: Citadel Press, 1962), and *New Guide to Rational Living* (North Hollywood: Wilshire Book Co., 1975).

2. David Burns, *Feeling Good* (New York: William Morrow and Co., 1980).

3. William Backus and Marie Chapian, *Telling Yourself the Truth* (Minneapolis: Bethany House Publishers, 1980).

4. David Stoop, *Self-Talk: Key to Personal Growth* (Old Tappan, N.J.: Fleming H. Revell, 1982).

Chapter 9 Intimacy: Leaving and Cleaving

1. Quoted by John Powell in *The Secret of Staying in Love* (Niles, Ill.: Argus Communications, 1974): 44.

2. David Augsburger, *Caring Enough to Forgive* (Ventura, Calif.: Regal Books, 1981). Lewis Smedes, *Forgive and Forget* (New York: Harper and Row, 1984).

3. Larry Day, "Couple Feeling-Word Activity" (201 Jefferson Bldg., 9370 S.W. Greenburg Rd., Portland, Ore. 97223).

4. John Powell, *The Secret of Staying in Love,* 73.

5. Jordan Paul and Margaret Paul, *Do I Have to Give Up Me to Be Loved by You?* (Minneapolis: CompCare Publishers, 1983), 210.

6. Edward Waring, *Enhancing Marital Intimacy through Cognitive Self-Disclosure* (New York: Brunner/Mazel Publishers, 1988).

7. Gary Smalley and John Trent, *The Language of Love* (Pomona, Calif.: Focus on the Family Publishing, 1988), 17.

Chapter 11 Confidentiality in Marriage Counseling

1. "Code of Ethics," American Association of Pastoral Counselors (Fairfax, Va., 1981): 2.

2. "Ethical Principles of Psychologists," *American Psychologist* 36, no. 6 (1981): 635–36.

Chapter 14 "To Everything There Is a Season"

1. Harvey L. Ruben, *Supermarriage: Overcoming the Predictable Crises of Married Life* (New York: Bantam Books, 1986), 9.

2. H. Norman Wright, *Seasons of a Marriage* (Ventura, Calif.: Regal Books, 1982).

3. Marvin Silberman and David Lustig, *Parent Survival Training* (North Hollywood: Wilshire Book Co., 1987). Earl D. Wilson, *Try Being a Teenager* (Portland, Ore.: Multnomah Press, 1982). Kevin Leman, *Parenthood Without Hassle* (Well, Almost) (Eugene, Ore.: Harvest House Publishers, 1979). James Dobson, *Parenting Isn't for Cowards* (Waco, Tex.: Word Books, 1987).

4. Emily Visher and John Visher, *Stepfamilies* (Secaucus, N.J.: Citadel Press, 1979).

5. Isalona Ricci, *Mom's House, Dad's House* (New York: Macmillan, 1980).

6. Ruben, *Supermarriage*, 25.

Chapter 15 Spouse Abuse

1. P. H. Neidig and D. H. Friedman, *Spouse Abuse: A Treatment Program for Couples* (Champaign, Ill.: Research Press Co., 1984): 5, 4.

2. Grant R. Martin, *Counseling for Family Violence and Abuse*, vol. 6 in Resources for Christian Counseling (Waco, Tex.: Word, 1987), 32–43.

3. Marie M. Fortune, *Keeping the Faith: Questions and Answers for the Abused Woman* (San Francisco: Harper and Row, 1987): 16–17.

4. J. D. Trotzer and T. B. Trotzer, *Marriage and Family: Better Ready Than Not* (Muncie, Ind.: Accelerated Development, 1986).

Chapter 16 Separation and Divorce

1. Harvey L. Ruben, *Supermarriage: Overcoming the Predictable Crises of Married Life* (New York: Bantam Books, 1986).
2. Andre Bustanoby, *But I Didn't Want a Divorce* (Grand Rapids: Zondervan Publishing House, 1978). Stanley A. Ellisen, *Divorce and Remarriage in the Church* (Grand Rapids: Zondervan Publishing House, 1977). Gary Richmond, *The Divorce Decision* (Waco, Tex.: Word Books, 1988).
3. Richard Krebs, *Alone Again* (Minneapolis: Augsburg Publishing House, 1978). Alan Loy McGinnis, *The Friendship Factor* (Minneapolis: Augsburg Publishing House, 1979). Harold Ivan Smith, *A Part of Me Is Missing* (Irvine, Calif.: Harvest House Publishers, 1979). Jim Smoke, *Growing through Divorce* (Eugene, Ore.: Harvest House Publishers, 1976) and *Living beyond Divorce: The Possibilities of Remarriage* (Eugene, Ore.: Harvest House Publishers, 1984). Anita Brock, *Divorce Recovery: Piecing Together Your Broken Dreams* (Fort Worth: Worthy Publishers, 1988).

Chapter 17 Termination of Counseling

1. Neil Jacobson, Lecture presented at the Helping People Change Conference (San Francisco, April 1988).

Chapter 18 Premarriage Counseling

1. Harold Bessell, *The Love Test* (New York: Warner Books, 1984).
2. G. Levinger and J. D. Snoek, *Attraction in Relationship: A New Look at Interpersonal Attraction* (Morristown, N.J.: General Learning Press, 1972).
3. B. I. Murstein, *Love, Sex, and Marriage Through the Ages* (New York: Springer, 1974).
4. E. M. Waring, *Enhancing Marital Intimacy through Facilitating Cognitive Self-Disclosure* (New York: Brunner-Mazel, 1988).

5. Clifford Sager, *Marriage Contracts and Couple Therapy* (New York: Brunner-Mazel, 1976).

6. DeLoss D. Friesen, *Marital Success Development Inventory* (201 Jefferson Bldg. 9370 S.W. Greenburg Rd., Portland, Ore. 97223).

7. David Olson, David Fournier, and Joan Druckman, Prepare-Enrich, Inc. (P.O. Box 190, Minneapolis, Minn. 55440, 1982).

8. Willard Harley, *His Needs, Her Needs* (Old Tappan, N.J.: Fleming H. Revell, 1986).

9. Bob Phillips, *How Can I Be Sure: A Pre-Marriage Inventory?* (Eugene, Ore.: Harvest House Publishers, 1978). Wes Roberts and H. Norman Wright, *Before You Say "I Do": A Marriage Preparation Manual for Couples* (Eugene, Ore.: Harvest House Publishers, 1978).

10. Peter L. Velander, *Remarriage: Challenge and Opportunity,* Shepherd's Staff, 346 Chester Street, St. Paul, Minn. 55107, 1985.

INDEX

Ruby M. Friesen, Ph.D.
DeLoss D. Friesen, Ph.D.

Ruby and DeLoss Friesen are affiliated with the Beaverton Family Counseling Center in Portland, Oregon. Ruby Friesen earned the master's and Ph.D. degrees in human development and counseling from the University of Nebraska and is a National Certified Counselor. Her husband DeLoss is a graduate of the University of Oregon and was professor of counseling psychology at the University of Nebraska before entering his present practice in 1977. He is a Diplomate in Counseling Psychology. The Friesens have taught marriage-enrichment seminars both locally and among American military personnel stationed in Europe. They are members of the Valley Community Presbyterian Church in Portland and are the parents of two grown children, Julie and Jeff.